The Beauty of the Mountain · Memories of J. Krishnamurti

The Beauty of the Mountain
Memories of J. Krishnamurti

Friedrich Grohe

Including the following quotations from Krishnamurti:

'Shall I talk about your teachings?'
'Brockwood Today and in the Future'
'The Intent of the Schools'
'The setting sun had transformed everything'
'Relationship with nature'
'Indifference and understanding'
'An idea put together by thought'
'Education for the very young'
'An extraordinary space in the mind'
'It is our earth, not yours or mine'
'The Core of K's Teaching'
'The Study Centres'
'Krishnamurti's Notebook – A Book Review'

KRISHNAMURTI FOUNDATIONS

Krishnamurti Foundation Trust Ltd
Brockwood Park, Bramdean, Hampshire SO24 0LQ, England
Tel: [44] (0)1962 771 525
info@kfoundation.org   www.kfoundation.org

Krishnamurti Foundation of America
P.O. Box 1560, Ojai, California 93024, USA
Tel: [1] (805) 646 2726
kfa@kfa.org   www.kfa.org

Krishnamurti Foundation India
Vasanta Vihar, 124 Greenways Road, RA Puram, Chennai 600 028, India
Tel: [91] 44 2 493 7803
info@kfionline.org   www.kfionline.org

Fundación Krishnamurti Latinoamericana
Calle Ernest Solvay 10, 08260 Suria (Barcelona), Spain
Tel: [34] 938 695 042
fkl@fkla.org   www.fkla.org

Additional Websites
www.jkrishnamurti.org   www.kinfonet.org

CONTENTS

ACKNOWLEDGEMENTS

I would like to thank Krishnamurti Foundation Trust Ltd and Krishnamurti Foundation of America for permission to publish material by and about Krishnamurti.

An earlier version of the chapter Last Journey to India was written as a contribution to Mary Lutyens's book *The Open Door*. It also appeared in Evelyne Blau's *Krishnamurti: 100 Years*.

Many friends helped in numerous ways with this labour of love and I thank them all. I am particularly grateful to the following for their input and assistance. Michael Krohnen, who translated most of the original German manuscript into English and who, because of his long acquaintance with Krishnamurti, was very helpful in working out ideas for the book. The late Mary Cadogan and the late Mary Lutyens. Nick Short, who edited the first edition; Claudia Herr, who edited subsequent editions; and Jürgen Brandt, who liaised with the designer and printers over successive editions. Nick, Claudia and Jurgen are colleagues in KLI (Krishnamurti Link International).

DEAR READER

This book came about because Krishnamurti asked the people who were working with him, the trustees for example, if we could convey the perfume of what it was like to be around him. At the same time, he didn't want us to be occupied with his personality but rather to use our energy to find out about ourselves. There are also comments and quotations by Krishnamurti included here that are not generally found elsewhere, in particular 'Brockwood Today and in the Future' and 'The Intent of the Schools', two statements that made me want to support this radical kind of education. They may be interesting and perhaps helpful for readers, and to collect them in a book was another incentive for me to write.

A friend once asked me what had touched me most about the teachings. After some reflection I realized it was something Krishnamurti had said during a public talk and also in one of the discussions with David Bohm[1] included in *The Ending of Time*. It was: *Love has no cause.* When people now ask me what Krishnamurti was like as a person, my first reply is that he was full of love and affection. It is clear to me that he lived what he was talking about. He was incredibly attentive and considerate and of course radically insightful. But I'm wary of reducing it, which is why I am including here virtually everything I remember – so one can get a general impression without (hopefully) my circumscribing it.

---

1 David Bohm was one of the most significant theoretical physicists of the 20th century. He had many recorded dialogues with K and, in 1969, was a founding trustee of Krishnamurti Foundation Trust Ltd (KFT) and Brockwood Park School in England. He died in 1992.

*View of the Rübli,
Videmanette, in Rougemont,
Switzerland*

The following excerpt from the book *Questions and Answers* led to the title *The Beauty of the Mountain*. It begins with a question that I could see myself asking Krishnamurti.

Shall I talk about your teachings?

QUESTION: I have understood the things we have talked over during these meetings, even if only intellectually. I feel they are true in a deep sense. Now when I go back to my country shall I talk about your teachings with friends? Or since I am still a fragmented human being will I only produce more confusion and mischief by talking about them?

KRISHNAMURTI: All the religious preachings of the priests, the gurus, are promulgated by fragmented human beings. Though they say, "We are high up," they are still fragmented human beings. And the questioner says: I have understood what you have said somewhat, partially, not completely; I am not a transformed human being. I understand, and I want to tell others what I have understood. I do not say I have understood the whole, I have understood a part. I know it is fragmented, I know it is not complete, I am not interpreting the teachings, I am just informing you what I have understood. Well, what is wrong with that? But if you say: "I have grasped the whole completely and I am telling you" then you become an authority, the interpreter; such a person is a danger, he corrupts other people. But if I have seen something which is true I am not deceived by it; it is true and in that there is a certain affection, love, compassion; I feel that very strongly – then naturally I cannot help but go out to others; it would be silly to say I will not. But I warn my friends, I say, "Look, be careful, do not put me on a pedestal." The speaker is not on a pedestal. This pedestal, this platform, is only for convenience; it does not give him any authority whatsoever. But as the world is, human beings are tied to something or other – to a belief, to a person, to an idea, to an illusion, to a dogma – so they are corrupt; and the corrupt speak and we, being also somewhat corrupt, join the crowd.

Seeing the beauty of these hills, the river, the extraordinary tranquility of a fresh morning, the shape of the mountains, the valleys, the shadows, how everything is in proportion, seeing all that, will you not write to your friend, saying, "Come over here, look at this"? You are not concerned about yourself but only about the beauty of the mountain.

Questions and Answers, pp. 63–64
3rd question & answer meeting, Saanen, July 1980
© 1982 Krishnamurti Foundation Trust Ltd

In these recollections I would like to share with my friends, and whoever else may be interested, *the beauty of the mountain.*

Friedrich Grohe,
Rougemont, Switzerland

INTRODUCTION

Over a period of more than seventy years Krishnamurti (K) gave thousands of public talks and discussions in many countries, but he never spoke a word too many. He was a genius of observation and of first-hand investigation into human consciousness. His speech was precise and clear and his appearance slim and well cared for. He was rather reserved, or, as he sometimes remarked, somewhat shy. Yet he would give his whole attention to whoever addressed him, taking an interest in all aspects and details. His love of life meant that anyone could approach him.

From 1983, when I first made K's acquaintance, I was in regular contact with him, accompanying him on many of his walks and travelling with him on his last journey to India; we would meet at Brockwood Park in England, Saanen in Switzerland, and Ojai in California. At Brockwood he arranged for me to have a room in the west wing, that part of the school complex where, since Brockwood's founding in 1969, he himself lived for three to four months each year.

K had been working during the first half of the 1980s to establish an adult study centre at Brockwood. He made a statement in 1983 titled 'Brockwood Today and in the Future', about the significance of Brockwood and the role of KFT in caring for it. In 1984 Mary Cadogan[2] gave me a copy of the statement. In my eyes

---

2 Mary Cadogan had been working for the BBC when, in 1958, she began her long association with K. She authored several books and in 2009 received an Honorary Doctor of Letters from Lancaster University, in part for her work with K. She was a KFT trustee from the beginning and until her death in 2014 at the age of 86. She leaves behind an unfinished book on K.

Trees in bloom, with the water tower behind them, at Brockwood Park

Brockwood was, and still is, a central part of K's legacy, and so, being further moved by what he had said, I offered to help with the study centre's funding. This allowed KFT to proceed with the project. K later told me, *Never give your capital away;* to which I replied, "Some has gone, but there is enough left to live on."

K was involved in choosing the site, the architect and some of the materials to be used. Of greatest importance, he made several statements about the intention of the place, what should happen there and its atmosphere. Among other things, he said: *You must plan fifty years ahead.* One of the most remarkable statements on this subject appears as Appendix 2 on pg. 96.

Around twenty architects submitted sketches and other work for the project, and six were felt to be outstanding. Eventually Keith Critchlow was chosen, a professor of sacred architecture and sacred geometry at the Royal College of Art in London. He gave a talk at Brockwood, which both K and I attended. I felt it was quite abstract and mentioned to K that I hadn't understood much of it. He admitted the same but added that he felt Critchlow was trying to find the root of architecture.

Construction began a few months after K's death and was completed at the end of 1987. K hadn't much liked the term 'adult study centre', expecting a better name could be found. In the end, it was left as simply 'study centre' (officially, The Krishnamurti Centre, Brockwood Park; more casually, the Centre).

In some ways, 'Brockwood Today and in the Future' applies to all of the Foundations in caring for the activities in their trust.

Brockwood Today and in the Future

For fourteen years Brockwood has been a school. It began with many difficulties, lack of money and so on, and we all helped to build it up to its present condition. There have been gatherings every year, seminars and all the activities of audio and video recording. We have reached a point now not only to take stock of what we are doing, but also to make Brockwood much more than a school. It is the only centre in Europe representing the Teachings, which are essentially religious. Though we have met in Saanen for the last twenty-two years for a month or more, Brockwood is the place where K spends much more time and energy. The school has a very good reputation and Mrs. Dorothy Simmons has put her great energy, her passion, behind it. We have all helped to bring the school about in spite of great difficulties, both financial and psychological.

Now Brockwood must be much more than a school. It must be a centre for those who are deeply interested in the Teachings, a place where they can stay and study. In the very old days an ashrama – which means retreat – was a place where people came to gather their energies, to dwell and to explore deeper religious aspects of life. Modern places of this kind generally have some sort of leader, guru, abbot or patriarch who guides, interprets and dominates. Brockwood must have no such leader or guru, for the Teachings themselves are the expression of that truth which serious people must find for themselves. Personal cult has no place in this. We must emphasize this fact.

Most unfortunately our brains are so conditioned and limited by culture, tradition and education that our energies are imprisoned. We fall into comforting and accustomed grooves and so become psychologically ineffective. To counter this we expend our energies in material concerns and self-centred activities. Brockwood must not yield to this well-worn tradition. Brockwood is a place for learning, for learning the art of questioning, the art of exploring. It is a place which must demand the awakening of that intelligence which comes with compassion and love.

It must not become an exclusive community. Generally, a community implies something separate, sectarian and enclosed for idealistic and utopian purposes. Brockwood must be a place of integrity, deep honesty and the awakening of intelligence in the midst of the confusion, conflict and destruction that is taking place in the world. And this in no way depends on any person or group of people, but on the awareness, attention and affection of the people who are there. All this depends on the people who live at Brockwood and on the Trustees of the Krishnamurti Foundation. It is their responsibility to bring this about.

So each one must contribute. This applies not only to Brockwood but to all the other Krishnamurti Foundations. It seems to me that one may be losing sight of all this, becoming engrossed in various demanding activities, caught up in particular disciplines, so that one has neither time nor leisure to be deeply concerned with the Teachings. If that concern does not exist, the Foundations have no significance at all. One can talk endlessly about what the Teachings are, explain, interpret, compare and evaluate, but all this becomes very superficial and really meaningless if one is not actually living them.

It will continue to be the responsibility of the Trustees to decide what form Brockwood should take in the future, but always Brockwood must be a place where integrity can flower. Brockwood is a beautiful place with old magnificent trees surrounded by fields, meadows, groves and the quietness of countryside. It must always be kept that way, for beauty is integrity, goodness and truth.

J. Krishnamurti
© 1983 Krishnamurti Foundation Trust Ltd

First Meetings with K

It was in 1980 that I first read a book by K: *The Impossible Question*, which I couldn't put down. It was like a revelation. I realized only later that his books can't be read as novels can. And it was the strangest thing: while he appeared to be saying the opposite of what I'd learned and experienced, he also seemed – in simple, clear and overwhelming language – to be saying what I'd always vaguely felt. He suggested in the book that we ask 'impossible questions' and the impossible question that he was asking was: *Can sorrow end?*

One of his most important statements, from his 1929 speech in Ommen, Holland, dissolving the Order of the Star in the East, is:

> I maintain that truth is a pathless land ...
> ... I am concerning myself with only one essential thing: to set man free. I desire to free him from all cages, from all fears, and not to found religions, new sects, nor to establish new theories and new philosophies.

This is the only statement of his that I can recall him referring to specifically. Normally he didn't refer back, nor did he quote other people.

Soon afterwards, someone told me that, each year, K gave a series of public talks in Saanen, Switzerland. Being quite content with studying his books, I had no desire to attend them. I also lost interest in, or perhaps simply understood the right place of, philosophy, psychology, literature, religion – and art, which had once captivated me – because I suddenly felt 'this is it!' The importance of understanding oneself was now so obvious that other people's books struck me as superfluous.

This was a time of great change for me. Besides other things, I was about to retire from business life. Previously I hadn't had much time to face essential questions, but now, all at once, K made it clear how important it was to concern oneself with central issues such as death and love, pleasure and pain, freedom, desire and fear. The more I explored the teachings, the more fascinating they became for me.

I attended the public talks at Saanen for the first time in 1981, usually walking there along the high road from my apartment in the neighbouring village of Rougemont. At an hour and a half, it takes longer than the river walk, and I would arrive just in time. Others would queue all night in order to have first choice at the seating once the giant tent was opened. The preferred seating was typically the floor space directly in front of the platform where K would speak, where every square meter was highly valued. In California and India, it was generally a bit more relaxed. I was happy to listen to K while sitting on the steps just inside the side entrance to the tent, which would always be full to capacity with around 3,000 people. There, I didn't have to sit amidst the crowd and, enjoying a fresh breeze, could be protected from the heat inside and outside the tent.

Afterwards it was possible to buy books by K translated into various languages, and I was glad to fill my rucksack with them. Having done so, however, and with that first summer being so hot (it was, I believe, 1983), on my hike back to Rougemont I would stop to cool off in the cold waters of the Grieschbach/ Fenils River.

It was overpowering to listen to K. He emanated so much energy that I felt I simply couldn't sit directly in front of him. He spoke simply and clearly, with few gestures and no rhetoric.

The view towards Saanen, with Rodomont in the background, from the bridge over the Saane that many people would have crossed while walking to the public talks

While listening, I would forget about food and drink and the heat. Afterwards I would feel light and inspired. Later I heard K asking people what happens to them after having been to the talks. They couldn't reply, so K spoke for them: *You become more sensitive.*

During one talk, I noticed an excited young man walking between the rows of people. He came along the long side of the tent where I was and proceeded to kick over a number of electric fans. As he came nearer, he gestured for me to move out of his way and I ducked, expecting a kick, although nothing of the sort came. Muttering curses, he continued walking towards K, on the way disdainfully flicking up a lady's necklace from which hung a portrait of the guru Rajneesh, also known as Osho. Proceeding to the platform, he grabbed the microphone from in front of K and started, in German, addressing K and the crowd. "The followers of Rajneesh should get out, they are not wanted here." Turning directly to K, he asked, "Am I not right, Mr. Krishnamurti? Don't you think so too?" The man appeared extremely agitated, even dangerous. Some of the people in the front row had jumped to their feet and one huge man, who resembled a wrestler, seemed to be on the point of throwing himself upon him. An atmosphere of violence flared up and an uproar followed. But just then K intervened, saying: *Don't touch him!* Apparently the intruder liked that, repeating, "Don't touch him, don't touch him." K nodded at him; the man finally calmed down, mumbled a few more words, and left the tent. K went on talking as if nothing had happened.

Another time, after a talk in Saanen as K was walking along the road to the car that was waiting for him, a tall male jogger came up beside him, looking rather disturbed or as though he wanted to annoy K. K abruptly lifted his head, and I had the impression that K's gaze was striking the man. The man staggered back.

It wasn't until 2011, when I handed a K book to an acquaintance from Gstaad who received the gift with scepticism, that I understood that residents in and around Saanen may have been influenced in their notion of Krishnamurti by the appearance of some of the attendees at the public talks. This acquaintance had been in her 20s when K gave his last talks at Saanen, in 1985, and all she remembered of the events were the large gatherings and some people in orange clothing – disciples sent by Rajneesh, who was claiming his message was the same as K's. Of course when K learned of Rajneesh's comparison he exclaimed: *It's exactly the contrary!* but my new friend wouldn't have known this. Instead, the orange clothing of a few, who had been going door to door distributing leaflets about Rajneesh, led her and probably others to suspect that a sect or cult was meeting in Saanen, an idea that would have horrified not only K but also most of those attending his talks.

K often spoke of the absurdity of having a guru. This didn't stop several gurus asking him to be their leader, however, which of course K refused. But later when a man came absolutely insisting, repeatedly, that K be his guru, K finally said: *Okay, I am your guru but you have to obey your guru.* After the man acquiesced, K went on: *I tell you you should never have a guru.* "But that's impossible," said the man. To which K replied: *Then I am not your guru.* He once told me: *Si on faisait un peu de cirque, on pourrait gagner beaucoup d'argent. (If we made some circus, we could earn lots of money.)*

There was another disruption, during one of the public talks at Ojai, when a young woman jumped onto the platform where K was sitting. He was startled but recovered immediately and told her that if she were willing to keep quiet he wouldn't mind her sitting next to him. She did indeed remain quiet, only occasionally rolling her head and grimacing. At the end of the talk, K bent towards her and said: *It is over.*

When I first attended the talks at Saanen, I didn't yet have contact with the Krishnamurti Foundations and Schools. I had read a statement in another book by K, *Education and the Significance of Life*, that said, in essence: If you are dissatisfied with the existing schools, why don't you start your own? This sounded perfectly reasonable and gave me the idea to start a school in Switzerland, where educators such as Piaget, Pestalozzi and Rousseau had been active. Thanks to the Krishnamurti Committee in Geneva informing me that a Brockwood teacher was about to return to her native Switzerland for the summer, I was able to contact Gisèle Balleys[3]. Soon afterwards she and I, together with several of her friends who were also interested in the project, began looking for a suitable building for a school. We found a very charming one at Chandolin, in the Valais. It was an old, well-preserved hotel, beautifully located with a distant view of the Matterhorn, and large enough to accommodate fifty to sixty students.

During the 1983 Saanen talks, K heard about this project from Gisèle and asked to meet me. He said: *I want to know this man.* At least that is how I've been remembering it. However, in the summer of 2015 during the Mürren Gathering, Gisèle told me the following: After I had contacted her about starting a school in Switzerland, she came to see me in Buchillon. Upon her approach she saw me working in the little garden I'd created there, wearing a green gardening apron. Rather doubtful that this was a man who could finance a school, she later told K of her impression. And this is when he asked her: *Do you want me to talk to this gentleman?*

---

3 Gisèle Balleys taught French for many years at Brockwood Park School. After K's death she began organizing gatherings in Saanen, which continue annually, now in Mürren, Switzerland. She oversees the French activities of the Krishnamurti Committee in Switzerland and she is a trustee of KFT.

In Matilija Canyon, Ojai

After the talks I rang Chalet Tannegg in nearby Gstaad, where he was staying, and it was agreed that we would meet there on August 1st. As I knew that K took particular care over his appearance, I went freshly shaved and well dressed. However, because the afternoons were quite hot, I had asked for a meeting in the morning, and when I arrived K was still in a simple tracksuit, for which he apologized. Even then I saw that he would enter a room quietly and gently, almost without notice.

I had brought two big bouquets, one for Mary Zimbalist[4] and one for K. Later I heard that he didn't like cut flowers, so the next year, when he was staying in Schönried, I sent an arrangement of living plants. These he appreciated.

K enjoyed speaking French and during this meeting and subsequent meetings we spoke French together. (We always addressed each other in the formal manner, using *vous*. He later told me that it took him a long time to *tutoyer*, to speak in familiar terms with someone, and I said that it was the same for me. In Mary Zimbalist's memoirs, she says it took K seven years to switch from calling her 'Mrs. Zimbalist' to 'Maria'.) In his caring way, he asked me about my life. We laughed and talked about mountain climbing – I was an enthusiastic alpinist – and a variety of other things. Pointing to the panorama outside I said, "I have climbed all the peaks in sight." He in turn pointed at the forests and hills and said: *And I have been on all the paths.* When I remarked that the mountains were really far more beautiful

---

4 Mary Zimbalist first heard of K in 1944 and began her association with him in 1965. For 21 years she was his personal secretary and travelling companion. She was a founding trustee of KFT and of Krishnamurti Foundation of America (KFA), established in California in 1973. She died in 2008 at the age of 93. Her memoirs are now freely available at inthepresenceofk.org; she also leaves behind an unfinished book about K. What she has written confirms to me the essence of my recollections about the time I spent with K.

Krishnamurti after a public talk at Brockwood Park, early 1980s

© *Vibeke Hovgaard*

from below than from above, he responded with a hearty *Yes!*

He asked me if I went up a mountain vertically or in a zigzag when ski-touring. He was impressed when I told him that I sometimes went up vertically. He mentioned that he would have liked skiing when he was younger but that he was not allowed to do it as it was considered too dangerous for him. He did, however, practice other kinds of sport. In his youth he played tennis, was an expert golfer, hiked, bicycled and swam. In his later life he would take brisk walks every day. And throughout his life he practiced yoga; in the last month of his life, his cook in India, Parameswaran, would be delighted each time he saw K doing his yoga exercises, as it confirmed he had regained some strength. I also mentioned that I'd often ridden a bicycle to my office at our factories. I'd hoped that some of the other employees might follow suit, but it never happened. K simply shook his head.

As a young man, K had visited Davos with some Dutch friends, and at Adelboden he lived in a mountain hut for some time. He told me he used to break the ice in the well every morning to have a wash, until he contracted bronchitis. He told me that in California he had once stayed in a hut all by himself. There had been a gramophone player there with a single record, Beethoven's Ninth Symphony. Every day he played it, until he knew every note by heart. He tended to be very receptive to music and was particularly fond of Bach, Beethoven, Mozart and other classical composers, as well as Sanskrit chanting and Indian classical music. I asked him once if he liked Chopin, thinking it might be too romantic, but he said he did. While K was staying in the hut in California, some people came and asked for the saint who was supposed to live there – he told them that the saint had just left. K had a great sense of humour, as I witnessed on many occasions.[5]

When we talked about the school that some of us wanted to start in Switzerland, K was emphatic: *You know how difficult it is to start a school? And they always need money.* "Well, I hope I'm not throwing my money out the window," I replied. K laughed heartily and added: *Before Brockwood, they had tried setting up a school in Switzerland, the Netherlands, France, Austria and Italy, but each time were unsuccessful.* Even since K's death, there have been attempts by others to start schools in Germany and other European countries; no new school has yet materialized. Some of those involved say it's because each person has his or her own idea about how things should be and, ultimately, the people can-

---

5 For example, Appendix 3, on pg. 100, is a book review, both funny and profound, of *Krishnamurti's Notebook*. The review was written by K himself.

Brockwood Park School

not work together. Additionally, as time goes on such projects become more and more expensive. There have, however, been four successful new schools in India.

The question of how to accomplish something good through the right use of money had been occupying my mind for some time. It had become clear that social and ecological organizations are quite limited in their capacity to bring about fundamental change; political or economic measures are unlikely to prevent mankind's destruction of nature. The only possibility is a deep change in the human psyche, together with the right kind of education – the intention of the various K Schools. So when

I asked K if he thought that money could do any good, his simple reply impressed me: *Someone once gave us some money, and with that money we bought Brockwood Park.*

Although K had warned me about the school project and had made it clear that, because he had enough on his plate with the existing Schools, 'Krishnamurti' couldn't be used in any new school's name, we continued with our plans.[6] It was difficult to find teachers for the new project, and there were hardly any prospective students, but we visited Brockwood to show K what we had accomplished so far. During lunch I tried to show him some photographs of Chandolin, but he wasn't interested in seeing them. Then he suddenly turned to Gisèle and asked her, while pointing at me: *He is the money. Would you build a school even without him?* Gisèle answered, "He isn't only the money." And K replied: *I know. I know.* He then turned to me and asked: *Do you have the right teachers, the right students and the right parents?* The scales fell from my eyes. We had nothing of the sort and it made no sense to start a new school; there were already Schools of the Krishnamurti Foundations in England, India and the USA. These K visited regularly, investing in them a lot of time and energy. It was clear to me that it was far more important to help the existing Schools with their financial and other difficulties than to start a new one.

Besides giving public talks to thousands of people, K would speak regularly with the students, teachers and staff of the Schools and Foundations, both individually and in groups. He had an extraordinary ability to solve practical problems, taking

---

6 Somewhat later I was amused to hear from Mark Lee that once, when K saw a new sign at Oak Grove School on which his name appeared rather prominently, he exclaimed: *The name [Krishnamurti] is too long and foreign. If I were a child, how could I tell my grandmother what school I went to?*

great care with all the details. He knew exactly where the real cause of a problem lay. I told him once that he would have been an excellent manager, had he opted for a business career. He laughed.

This exchange occurred after I had got to know him a little better. But already during our first encounters he showed himself to be a flexible, open-minded person with a great sense of humour, a man of modesty and genuine kindness. I was very much interested in how a person with such overwhelming insight into life lived his daily life, what kind of person he was. Didn't he have worries and longings? Wasn't he ever angry, anxious or aggressive? One couldn't imagine how a human being without ego – as he was – could live in this world. Mary Zimbalist once said to me that K led a very simple life. From what I knew of him, this struck me as accurate.

Mary Lutyens[7] in her biographies of K approached the larger question of *who* K was. While K often emphasized that who he was is unimportant – what is far more important is who *you* are – he also spoke powerfully about this question.[8]

---

7 Mary Lutyens was a young child when she first met K soon after his arrival in England. Her mother, Lady Emily Lutyens (wife of the architect Sir Edwin Lutyens) was very close to K for many years. K asked Mary to write his biography, which led to *The Years of Awakening, The Years of Fulfilment, The Open Door* and *The Life and Death of Krishnamurti*. After reading the first edition of *The Beauty of the Mountain*, she commented that K felt alive in it. She died in 1999 at the age of 90.

8 For more on the matter, see *Krishnamurti's Notebook, Krishnamurti's Journal*, Mary Lutyens's biographies and the other books listed on pp. 107–108.

VISIT TO BUCHILLON

In August 1984, on his way from Saanen to Geneva Airport, K visited me in Buchillon, the village beside Lake Geneva where I was living. We met at the beautiful courtyard of nearby Château d'Allaman, with its magnificent trees. K got into my car, while Mary Zimbalist and Dr. Parchure[9], who were accompanying him, followed in their car. During the drive to Buchillon, we came through a forest that had been the site of a Roman necropolis. At some point, I had the sensation that there was no one sitting beside me. While I felt I might be disturbing him, I also wanted to check on him and so asked whether he was familiar with the area. He answered immediately, but I had the feeling that he'd returned from a remote place in order to do so.

Several people told me later that they had had similar experiences with K. Whenever he declared later *I am nobody*, I was reminded of this incident. Dr. Parchure told me that K was at home in two dimensions: our daily existence and a different dimension altogether.

On many occasions K remarked that he had hardly any memory of the past, and that not carrying the burden of it gave him tremendous energy. At Rishi Valley in India we once met an old man who insisted that he had known K for many years. K did not remember him and afterwards said to me: *Tout le monde connaît le singe, mais le singe ne connaît personne. (Everyone knows the monkey, but the monkey doesn't know anyone.)*

---

9 Dr. T. K. Parchure accompanied K on his travels in India from 1973 onwards in order to look after K's health. In the later years he also attended to K in Europe and the USA, and was present at K's death at Ojai in 1986.

Lake Geneva, at Buchillon, Switzerland. Once, after I had returned from a visit to Buchillon, K asked me: How was it? When I started to reply, "The lake was ...," he completed the sentence quicker than I could think: ... comme un mirroir (... like a mirror).

After arriving at Buchillon we went down to the lake. K stopped on the path under the trees, listened and said just one word: *Silence.* I felt he was referring not just to external silence. There was a broken branch on the path that he carefully put to one side. He had a look at the irrigation system and immediately discerned how it functioned. He recognized the monkey puzzle tree (Araucaria araucana) in front of the house, though it's quite exotic, and pointed out to Mary the particularly beautiful dark violet-blue petunias blooming on the balcony, which I had been tending. By the lakeside he told me how, in 1920, he and his brother had spent a holiday across the lake at Amphion, between Thonon and Evian: the Hôtel des Princes had been uncomfortable, with too little hot water to warm themselves after a cold swim in the lake. He assumed this was the cause of his brother's tuberculosis, which led to his early death at Ojai in 1925.

A year later, on his way to Saanen, K stopped for lunch at Buchillon. As he entered the dining room, he exclaimed *Huh!* and for a moment covered his eyes with one hand. There were at that time a number of strongly coloured paintings on the wall, some of them of half-naked women; during the meal he carefully regarded the one hanging in front of him. Whenever K looked at something, he did so intensely and for a long time. He told me how, before the war, in Paris, he was shown Picasso's painting Guernica. After looking at it for quite a while, he had asked: *What is this all about?* Goya was an artist whom K appreciated, perhaps among other reasons because of Goya's claim to have been still learning at the age of 90, but he felt that modern artists only increased the general confusion and division by expressing chaos, aggressiveness and fragmentation. When I subsequently returned to Brockwood, Dorothy Simmons[10] reported that K had spoken enthusiastically about his visit to the house at Buchillon.

While at Brockwood I was invited to attend the meetings of K with the staff and students. Almost everyone would look terribly serious when K entered the room. He would then sit in front of the assembly and, to begin with, gaze at each person one by one. As I felt so happy to be invited, I gave him a big smile when he looked at me. Radiantly, he smiled back, in a way no one had ever

---

10 Dorothy Simmons was a recognized sculptress and educator before helping to set up Brockwood Park School in 1969, along with her husband, Montague. She was the School's first principal and a trustee until her death in 1989. She was and still is highly regarded by many former students and staff members, and K once told me that they could establish Brockwood because of the liberal school system in England and because they had found the right person to head it.

From Buchillon, Switzerland, a view over Lake Geneva towards Amphion

The Hôtel des Princes in Amphion, France, today; where K stayed in 1920

done towards me before. The people in front turned around to see what was going on!

An exchange during one of these discussions (on 16 October 1983) I remember well, because there was so much laughter. One of the boys claimed he understood what was being said about intelligence but, nevertheless, didn't feel he was becoming more intelligent. Frustrated, he asked another student what intelligence meant to her. She evaded the question, pointing to K and simply saying she believes what he says, which made people laugh. K went on: *Let's take another thing, perhaps that will explain it.* The girl interjected, "But if he can't see that one, is he going to see? If he can't see that as intelligence, what can he see?" K laughingly told the boy: *She is insulting you!* He said it in such a generous way that everyone was very much amused.

Suprabha Seshan[11], a long-time friend, recalls that when she was a student at Brockwood K once asked her: *Why do you want to go to university? What about this land here, isn't it all here?* On another occasion, he said to her: *Throw it all away, question everything, challenge the speaker, ask deeply What is the root of your conditioning, how were you brought up, what happened to you when you were very young, how did your parents and teachers raise you?* When she later told him that she was going to university, he asked: *Do you think you will be more intelligent after that?*

---

11 Suprabha Seshan is an 'ecosystem gardener', ecologist, educator and writer, who for many years has helped to run the internationally renowned Gurukula Botanical Sanctuary in Kerala, India, winning the Whitley Prize in 2006. She was a Rishi Valley, Valley School and Brockwood student.

O JAI

In May 1984 I went to Ojai for the public talks. It's sometimes claimed that 'Ojai' (pronounced O-high) means 'nest', and indeed there is a great sense of peace pervading the whole valley. Arriving from Ventura one feels it, particularly at dusk or during one of the magnificent moonlit nights that occur there. The name 'Ojai' actually comes from the Chumash word meaning 'moon'.

Returning regularly, K spent a great part of his life at Ojai, and it was there in 1925 that death claimed his brother, and in 1986 K himself.

Wherever K made his home, he would invite to lunch friends and other interesting people with whom he wanted to converse.[12] This was the custom at Saanen, Madras (now Chennai), Rishi Valley, Rajghat at Varanasi on the Ganges, and Ojai. At Brockwood there were fewer guests, because he lunched in the dining room with students and staff. Michael Krohnen[13], who had been taught

---

12 As Asit Chandmal, a nephew of Pupul Jayakar (see footnote 32 on pg. 55) who knew K from childhood, wrote at the beginning of his book *One Thousand Suns*, K once said to him: *I wish you could travel with me, and meet the variety of people I see. Doctors, writers, scientists, artists, so-called religious men, philosophers, wives and mothers and husbands, clerks, bureaucrats and their bosses.*

13 Michael Krohnen, originally from Germany, worked as chef at Oak Grove School and in various capacities for KFA. He was K's cook in Ojai for many years and is the author of *The Kitchen Chronicles: 1001 Lunches with J. Krishnamurti.* He now runs the Krishnamurti Library at Pine Cottage, K's Ojai residence.

to cook by Alan Hooker[14], was the chef at Ojai. In addition to preparing meals, it was Michael's informal duty during lunches to keep K up to date with the news of the world. Michael was naturally well suited to the task; also, he had a strong voice and K had become slightly deaf in his last years. On one occasion, K laughingly told me: *First the teeth, then the ears, then the eyes, and then down to earth.* Another time, during a public talk, he quoted an Italian proverb: *Everybody has to die; perhaps me, too.*

At Ojai, when arriving for lunch, he would go to the kitchen first – peeping into the pots and exchanging a few words with Michael – and then enter the dining room from there. Michael and I once calculated how many times K had stepped through that kitchen door, and reckoned it must have been close to a thousand while Michael was chef.

Michael invited me to join him when receiving K in the kitchen, and K and I, too, would exchange a few words. One day, burdened with marriage difficulties, I decided to ask K for help, but not out loud. I was simply thinking, "Please help!" On this occasion, however, K completely ignored me. I thought perhaps he didn't get my message but I also wondered if his indifference might be intentional. And of course now when I think back, I realize that whenever I tried to put myself in the foreground he ignored me; he became almost neutral, almost absent; one couldn't reach him. It was a good lesson not to ask for help.

Though there were sometimes as many as twenty guests for lunch, K was actually rather shy. Once, when a great number had

---

14 Alan Hooker was the founding owner of the famous Ranch House Restaurant in Ojai. His association with K began in 1949 and he was a trustee of KFA until 1989. On K's suggestion, he wrote what is said to be the first vegetarian cookbook in the US; it became a best-seller and is still in print. He died in 1993 at the age of 90. His wife, Helen Hooker, was also a trustee of KFA. She died in 2000 at the age of 97.

come, I heard him enquiring: *Who are all those people?* He would approach the crowd unseen, modestly stepping out from behind a screen and inviting the guests with *Madame est servie.*

Lunch at Ojai was a self-service buffet, and after the meal everyone would take his or her dishes to the kitchen for cleaning. K would serve himself last and, afterwards, carry to the kitchen not only his dishes but often also some of the pots, sometimes the biggest ones.

During one of these lunches, K mentioned a statement about Oak Grove School that he had written in 1975 and later revised with the school staff; he wished it to be distributed during the public talks. The Foundation lacked a good copier, however, and it looked as though it would be difficult to print the statement in time. In response, I made a donation to the Foundation of a high-quality photocopier, and 'The Intent of Oak Grove School' – later called 'The Intent of the Schools', since it applies to all of them – was distributed.

The Intent of the Schools

It is becoming more and more important in a world that is destructive and degenerating that there should be a place, an oasis, where one can learn a way of living that is whole, sane and intelligent. Education in the modern world has been concerned with the cultivation, not of intelligence, but of intellect, of memory and its skills. In this process little occurs beyond passing information from the teacher to the taught, the leader to the follower, bringing about a superficial and mechanical way of life. In this there is little human relationship.

Surely a school is a place where one learns about the totality, the wholeness of life. Academic excellence is absolutely necessary, but a school includes much more than that. It is a place where both the teacher and the taught explore not only the outer world, the world of knowledge, but also their own thinking, their behavior. From this they begin to discover their own conditioning and how it distorts their thinking. This conditioning is the self to which such tremendous and cruel importance is given. Freedom from conditioning and its misery begins with this awareness. It is only in such freedom that true learning can take place. In this school it is the responsibility of the teacher to sustain with the student a careful exploration into the implications of conditioning and thus end it.

A school is a place where one learns the importance of knowledge and its limitations. It is a place where one learns to observe the world not from any particular point of view or conclusion. One learns to look at the whole of man's endeavor, his search for beauty, his search for truth and for a way of living without conflict. Conflict is the very essence of violence. So far education has not been concerned with this, but in this school our intent is to understand actuality and its action without any preconceived ideals, theories or belief which bring about a contradictory attitude toward existence.

The school is concerned with freedom and order. Freedom is not the expression of one's own desire, choice or self-interest. That inevitably leads to disorder. Freedom of choice is not freedom, though it may appear so; nor is order conformity or imitation. Order can only come with the insight that to choose is itself the denial of freedom.

In school one learns the importance of relationship which is not based on attachment and possession. It is here one can learn about the movement of thought, love and death, for all this is our life. From the ancient of times, man has sought something beyond the materialistic world, something immeasurable, something sacred. It is the intent of this school to inquire into this possibility.

The Pepper Tree in front of Pine Cottage, K's home in Ojai. A few years ago the Pepper Tree fell, but new shoots have grown out of the huge trunk that remained and it is once again vigorous and beautiful.

This whole movement of inquiry into knowledge, into oneself, into the possibility of something beyond knowledge, brings about naturally a psychological revolution, and from this comes inevitably a totally different order in human relationship, which is society. The intelligent understanding of all this can bring about a profound change in the consciousness of mankind.

J. Krishnamurti
© 1981 Krishnamurti Foundation Trust Ltd

During this period, as in other years, K held several dialogues at Oak Grove School and at Pine Cottage – his home in Ojai from 1922 until his death – with teachers, trustees and occasionally parents. During one of these discussions, at Pine Cottage, he asked David Moody[15]: *Do you trust Mr. Grohe?* David replied, "I don't know him." K responded: *You see! You see!* Ivan Berkovics[16] has reminded me that K then leaned towards me and said: *It's not personal.* K was always stressing that real trust is not dependent on the knowledge one has of another person. Mary Cadogan once told me that K had said to her: *You can trust Mr. Grohe.* Similarly, I don't believe that my attitude regarding the teachings would be any different if I had never met K personally.

I realize while writing this that my feeling for K was one of complete trust, and it remains so – and this is also why I have wanted to support the work. I think K understood this. He once asked me: *Why are you giving us all this money?* I didn't know what to reply, so he replied for me, lifting up his arms: *Ça vient tout seul! (It comes on its own!)* It's also what he said, according to friends, on an occasion when he happened to see me: *He wants to help.*

By spring of the following year, 1985, I had purchased a house in Ojai. I'd first looked at the so-called Radix Institute, above the Oak Grove at the top of Besant Road (where the Ojai Retreat now is). I told K about this and mentioned that the atmosphere wasn't good, to which he responded: *Let's be there for a while.* I ended up buying another house, on Country Club Drive. While it was

---

15 David Moody was the first teacher hired at Oak Grove School and was later its educational director, then director of the school. He co-authored *Mapping Biology Knowledge* (Kluwer, 2000) and authored *The Unconditioned Mind – J. Krishnamurti and the Oak Grove School* (see pg. 76).

16 Ivan Berkovics taught at Wolf Lake School (a K School in Victoria, B.C., Canada, that ran for a few years in the late 1970s/early 1980s and is now the Swanwick Centre) and at Oak Grove School in Ojai; he also worked for KFA. He is now a substitute/supply teacher and he runs Lindley House, a guest house beside KFA's Pepper Tree Retreat.

being refurbished, I stayed for almost two weeks at Arya Vihara, where the lunches were held. This is where Annie Besant[17] and also Aldous Huxley[18] had stayed, and where K's brother Nitya had died. It is a large but simple and very well kept house surrounded by flowers, flowering shrubs and splendid great trees, with a wonderful atmosphere. Having served for many years after K's death as the Krishnamurti Library, it is now KFA's Pepper Tree Retreat. The Krishnamurti Library & Visitor Center is next door at Pine Cottage.

When K came to visit the house on Country Club Drive, he admired the trees the most. He was no longer in the best of health but still very active. At one point, when we happened to be standing outside, I mentioned a feeling, experienced by several people, that there was a ghost in the house, especially in the guest room and also around the fireplace in the living room. I asked K if he could do anything about it. He requested that we wait outside. On one of the following days he asked me in a modest and friendly way: *Did you feel something?* At first I didn't know what he meant, but then realized, "Ah, you mean the ghost. Oh, yes, it's wonderful – such peace, such tremendous quiet. But I wonder if this is just imagination." K grabbed my arm with his usual intensity and said: *So do I.*

---

17 Annie Besant (1847–1933) was President of the Theosophical Society from 1907 to 1933. She adopted K and his brother Nityananda in 1909. A famous and outstanding public speaker, she was active in the early women's movements and also in the movement for Indian independence. She remained closely associated with K until her death and was always greatly respected by him.

18 Aldous Huxley, the well-known author – *Brave New World, Island, Eyeless in Gaza, Crome Yellow*, among others – met K in California in 1938. He encouraged K in his writing and wrote the Introduction to K's *The First and Last Freedom*. They remained close friends until Huxley's death in 1963.

The house had a separate small apartment. One day K asked if we could house Bill Quinn[19] there, a friend of the Foundation. When we agreed, K jumped happily into the air.

K liked to visit the Lilliefelts[20] at their house on Grand Avenue. During one visit, he spoke of his body, saying that it should have been dead long ago. Pointing to the sky, he claimed: *They did something up there.*

One time I was at Pine Cottage with K, Mary, the Lilliefelts and Mark Lee[21], a day after K had been to Los Angeles with Mary. He said: *We were so tired that we went to bed at 9 o'clock.* There followed a silence during which the unspoken question must have become clear to K, because he then added, to much laughter: *But not together.*

Another time K told me that in his younger years he'd gone to a party in Hollywood. At some point a lady invited him to dance. In his jovial and slightly embarrassed way, he said that she was so big he couldn't get his arm around her.

---

19 In the 1940s Bill Quinn spent a year at Arya Vihara, tending the grounds. K was at Pine Cottage during that time and they often worked together in the garden and looking after the cow, chickens and bees. Bill was later one of the founders of the Esalen Institute at Big Sur, California, and he worked on the first Krishnamurti Index of subjects that became KFT's three-volume Index of all of the audio- and videotapes. He died in Ojai in 1998.

20 Erna and Theo Lilliefelt had known K since the early 1950s and were founding trustees of KFA. Erna played a crucial role in the recovery of assets for KFA from Rajagopal, a long-time organizer of K's talks and publications whose daughter, Radha Sloss, went on to write a defamatory book on K. Theo died in 1998 and Erna in 2002; both were over 90.

21 Mark Lee had been head of the junior school at Rishi Valley and was the first director of Oak Grove School. He is a retired Executive Director of KFA and continues to be a trustee. He gives lectures and seminars worldwide on various topics informed by K's teachings.

The oak tree near Pepper Tree Retreat (Arya Vihara) in Ojai, California, under which K wrote Education and the Significance of Life *in the early 1950s*

At one of the lunch meetings with K at Arya Vihara, some of us, including Radha Burnier[22], were discussing pollution, the waste of paper represented by Sunday newspapers that are as big as books, and the horror of slaughterhouses. After listening attentively to what we were talking about, K said: *Yes, this is all terrible. But it's secondary.* With great emphasis he added: *Why does man kill man?!*

At another lunch, I told K that I had allowed a psychiatrist friend from Lausanne to use my house at Buchillon for a conference with other psychiatrists. He examined the programme with great care, as he did everything brought to his attention. His comment: *Nothing but words. Nothing about their own lives.* Similarly, he would sometimes remark about modern-day philosophy that most of it amounted to just *more talk about talk, and more words about words and books written about books written by someone else.*

It was with laughter that K told the story of his encounter with the multi-millionaire in Washington, D.C. (It was 1985 and K was giving two days of talks at the Kennedy Center.) Immediately upon sitting down, the man declared, "I believe in Jesus Christ." K responded by asking: *Why do you believe?* and involved him in a discussion on the reasons behind looking for security in a belief. The man's face became harder and harder, like the brick wall behind him.

In Washington, the superpower capital, K stated publicly: *Power is an ugly thing … in any form.* In India he remarked to me that he did not like the atmosphere in Delhi, as it was a seat of power.

---

22 Radha Burnier met K when she was very young, and they remained warm friends until the end of K's life. She was President of the Theosophical Society from 1980 until her death, at age 90, in 2013. She was also a trustee of Krishnamurti Foundation India (KFI), which was established in 1928.

BROCKWOOD PARK

At the beginning of June 1984, K and Mary Zimbalist and I flew from Los Angeles to London, to go to Brockwood. Mark Lee, who was taking us to the airport, had to drive flat out when we realized we'd misread our departure time. It turned out, however, that our flight had been delayed.

Because of K's advanced age, and at the Foundations' insistence, he was travelling first class. I had tried to book first class too but, with no more seats available, was flying business. K had declared: *We shall do something about your ticket.* I didn't know what he meant, and had forgotten about it. When the time came, K and Mary checked in and then went on ahead, leaving me to check in. Once I had done so, and was following, one of the staff came running after me with a new ticket – for a seat in first class directly behind K, without my having to pay anything more.

On our arrival in London, one of K's bags failed to show up. I was impressed by how patiently he waited until there was no more luggage and the conveyor belt stopped; he reported the difficulty without making a fuss, and his bag was eventually tracked down and sent to him.

Another example of this warm indifference to waiting was when we were sitting in a car by the west wing at Brockwood, waiting to go to the airport together. We had to wait quite a long time for Mary Zimbalist, and one might expect that K would have been nervous at the prospect of such a long journey. But he sat and waited with complete composure and was even cheerful, though it was a long wait. Some time later Mary told me that K always left far too early for airports. One time I said to him, "The faster we can go, the less time we have." His only reply was: *More, more, more!*

Since the late 1960s/early '70s, once Brockwood had been set up as a school, K had the following regular schedule for his travels: after the public talks at Ojai and sometimes US cities such as Los Angeles, San Francisco, New York, Washington, D.C., Los Alamos, he would go to Brockwood, around mid-May, where he was always full of energy and worked passionately with the students and especially with the staff on what to do at the School; at the end of June, just as the school year was ending, he would leave for the public talks at Saanen and return to Brockwood for the public talks there in September; he would go to India early in November, visiting all the Schools and giving public talks at Madras, Bombay (now Mumbai), and Rajghat; he would leave India in February to go to Ojai, stopping over at Brockwood for a few days. Then the cycle would begin again. In 1984, during his brief stopover at Brockwood, it was especially cold, with unusual ice and snow, and he still went for a walk, although he was blue with cold afterwards. I mentioned to him that most of the time he arrived at a place in springtime, so that he had an eternal spring.[23] He smiled at this.

As we flew over the California desert there was a magnificent sunset below. The mountains were glowing in all shades and colours, from the deepest purple to the most delicate pink. We could see the straight lines of roads and railroad tracks cutting through the desert. When we arrived in England, K enthusiastically called out: *Look at it, just look. All this green!*

At Brockwood I stayed in the west wing in a small room with a balcony. When K first showed me the room, he said: *Here you*

---

23 For example, Rishi Valley has spring in December, and in Saanen's high mountains spring comes in June.

The Krishnamurti Centre at Brockwood Park, springtime

are at home. The balcony was reached by climbing through the window. Having cleared away the dirt of generations, an expression K agreed with, and after wrapping myself in my coat and several blankets, I practiced my yoga exercises there in the mornings, even when it was still dark. K found the whole thing quite fascinating and took a good look at the balcony. Someone once took a photograph of my feet projecting above the balustrade while I was doing a headstand.

K practiced yoga throughout his life. He emphasized that it was good for the body but that it had nothing to do with spiritual enlightenment. He also said that yoga was quite different in earlier times, being only for the few.

Sometimes, when K would show me yoga exercises, I wondered what his state of mind was while doing them. There was an atmosphere of intensity that is difficult to describe. It seemed as if his whole personality was absent, but at the same time one could feel an enormous presence.

Punctually at 7 a.m. we would do the yoga exercises and also various breathing, eye, and neck and shoulder exercises, ending with jogging and jumping on the spot.[24] K was still doing all of this at the age of 89. He was so dynamic and young in his whole attitude, and his energy was that of a young person, that I was not sensitive to his age. I suggested that we also do other yoga exercises in the evening, never thinking that he might get tired.

The breathing exercises alone took about half an hour, and when K first told me that he would teach them to me, he added: *Then you can walk.* In fact, I was already accustomed to long hikes, as well as to mountain climbing and alpine ski-touring. During the last summer with K at Rougemont, I would set out early in the morning, partly to escape the heat of the day. When I returned for lunch, K would ask me: *Combien d'heures? (How many hours?)* I would answer three, four or five hours; he was always impressed and eventually concluded: *He wants to go on walking until the end of his days.*

After our yoga exercises one morning, K pulled up the blinds in his room, thereby opening up a magnificent view of the pastures and distant hills. Pointing at this beauty, he said to me in Latin: *Benedictus est qui venit in nomine domini.* He asked me to translate, which I did as "Blessed is he who comes in the name of God." When I pronounced the word 'God', he dismissed it with

---

24 His eyesight was so good that he never needed glasses. Later we wrote down all of the exercises so that I could do them on my own.

a gesture. K often pointed out that God, especially when given a human form, was an invention of the human mind.

Another morning, as I arrived for the yoga, K's room was still in darkness and he was in bed. On my opening the door, he woke immediately and said: *Today I shall stay in bed the whole day.* I replied, "Good night," and he laughed. He had been to London the day before and the city always exhausted him. Once after returning from London he met me on the stairs, and we both wondered why one went to such a place. He said it was a relief to get out of it again, which was exactly how I felt. But Mary Zimbalist's memoirs make clear that during the 1970s K travelled to London frequently from Brockwood, more than once a week even. Such trips would have been calmer then: easy to find a parking place when going by car and less crowded when going by train. And, wherever he was, he enjoyed going to the cinema.

One of the things that amazed me about K was the natural joy he had in physical contact: holding hands, hugging, just a little touch with its healing power. For me, hugging was not a natural way of greeting someone or bidding farewell; I was more used to the French or Swiss way of kissing cheeks. I never saw K kissing: he hugged, and as I didn't know how to do this properly, we sometimes got entangled. I learned it eventually at Rajghat, witnessing the easy way that K greeted Michael Krohnen. Surprised to see him there, K threw his arms in the air and hugged so readily – and Michael was substantially taller and wider than K. As can be seen in the photo on the back cover, K and I were almost the same size, only his arms and feet were longer.

I remember my astonishment when, while showing me breathing exercises, K asked me to put my hand on his abdomen to feel the movement of his inhalations and exhalations. It felt as if his lungs would fill the whole of his abdomen, so deep and free was his breathing.

At Brockwood K always insisted on rinsing his own dishes after meals and if anyone offered to help him, he'd reply: *It's my job.* He also insisted on cleaning his own shoes. On one occasion I saw him polishing the west wing banister with great enthusiasm. *In India they would never allow me to do that.* There he was obliged to let the servants wait on him. Nevertheless, for many years at Rishi Valley he had a very small room, which he said he didn't mind at all. *I simply looked out the window,* he joked. At Tannegg, the rented chalet in Gstaad where I first met him, he once told me that he and Mary Zimbalist didn't go into Gstaad any longer, because it had become *trop mondain (too high-society or too fashionable).*

Raman has told me that during a dialogue with teachers and guests at Rishi Valley, K asked a question that resulted in a long silence from everyone. Looking around, he finally said: *Where have all the intellectual birds gone now?* He then caught Raman's eye and added: *Don't mind Raman and me, we're just the cooks.*

He was fascinated with technical things. In his younger years he could repair cars and it's often reported that he dismantled a watch and put it together again. Knowing he liked such things, and that he used an electric shaver, I once gave him a new kind of Braun shaver, very small. He grabbed it and ran away with it excitedly. When, in Ojai, K sat in my new BMW to have a look at it, he asked: *What are all these buttons for?* I couldn't tell him – there were too many and I didn't know.

There were times when I ate with K, Mary and others in the small west wing kitchen at Brockwood. On one such occasion someone raised the topic of national characteristics and everyone contributed observations. When it came to the British, I said "fair play". K was sitting beside me and pulled me aside a bit, saying: *But not with the Indians.* On another occasion, he accidentally knocked over a glass of water, after which he stated emphatically: *Dreaming!* Once at lunch in Ojai he happened to

The two pine trees remaining, with one ready to fall, of the several that K said we should not disturb while we walked at Brockwood Park

drop something. In response to my slightly astonished look, he explained: *This always happens before a talk.*

He was a modest person, very gentle in his personal dealings and extremely courteous. Towards women he was most considerate, even chivalrous. I recall one lunch at Brockwood during which an elderly woman from Paris, who must have known K for quite some time, expressed how terribly afraid she was of dying. K said in French something like: *No, no – don't worry. Everything will be fine.* Much later I heard that she had died peacefully.

He occasionally expressed irritation with some men's attitude towards women: *How you look at women!* One day I was walking beside him and a very attractive woman came towards us. Bearing in mind his admonition, I didn't know what to do:

should I look or not? And then I saw that K was looking at her very intensely.

Once Dr. Shirali[25] walked by with his wife two meters behind him. K stopped them and said to her: *Now you walk in front and he walks behind.*

There were occasions when he would be impatient with someone, but he never wanted to hurt anyone's feelings or tell anyone directly what to do, though I felt that he did on occasion make an impersonal comment that nevertheless seemed meant for a particular person. There was a sense of love about him. He would point at the deeper causes of the problem at hand and urge the person to find for him- or herself the right action. One could learn something from every word he uttered.

In 1984 there were great difficulties at Brockwood concerning the direction of the School. One group within the staff was in conflict with another, leading to some people leaving. K devoted his whole energy to the problem. Several times he spoke to the entire staff. Once he even threatened to close the door to the west wing and never set foot in the School again. Naturally, he also spoke to the students, and he was shocked when they told him that the teachers and other staff members were spending very little time with them, preoccupied as they were with their own difficulties. He then spoke to the adults in an unusually strict way. We seemed to have run into each other outside the assembly hall immediately after the meeting, but he must have detected me in the crowd. He took my hand while we went for a short walk, and told me: *I have never talked like this before.* I was glad I wasn't a staff member. But Raman

---

25 Shailesh Shirali, a long-time mathematics teacher at Rishi Valley School who was for several years also the principal there, is now a KFI trustee and the education director at Sahyadri School, a K School near Pune begun after K's death.

Patel[26], who was also in the meeting, has told me that he never felt any pressure from K, because what K had to say was never personal.

K once told me that a teacher at Rajghat claimed, "When you come here it's like a thunderstorm, and we are glad when you leave." This reminds me of K saying: *Nothing grows under the banyan tree.* It's a south Indian proverb, and I've always felt he meant by it that we would see what insight and strength we were capable of only after he was gone.

Many people who came to K's public talks said that he would raise the very topic they were most interested in at the time. Since K often addressed thousands of people, one has to ask how such a thing was possible. Was the same problem on everyone's mind? Was it common consciousness, which we all share? Does each problem contain every other problem, like a hologram? Did we understand at all what he was talking about? Once, after one of the public talks at Brockwood, we were walking over the south lawn towards the west wing when a young man approached. Addressing K, he began trying to summarize the talk, presumably to lead into a question. K, having said nothing like what the young man was describing, gently explained it again, then added that they couldn't discuss it there and then and that the young man should come another time.

Mary Cadogan has told me that she once remarked to K, "You take away our crutches before we can walk." His reply was: *Yes, and then you will learn to fly.*

---

26 Raman Patel was a staff member at Brockwood for 15 years and continues his involvement there, and with KFI, in a consulting capacity. He works with Krishnamurti Link International (see pg. 89), among other things travelling throughout the world to foster contact among those who are interested in K's teachings. He helped to build up Stream Garden Retreat Centre in southern Thailand.

And Mary Zimbalist once told me that when K wasn't satisfied with the written questions handed in for the public question and answer meetings, which followed the public talks, he would write some of them himself.

From my room in the west wing I could sometimes hear what was going on in the small kitchen there. K was talking a lot with Scott Forbes[27], in the evenings, which he later described as *cooking* Scott for his job as principal.

In K's company, the perception of the natural beauty around Brockwood was more intense. On walks, he would talk very little. When crossing pastures, he insisted that one not use shortcuts. *Don't cut corners!* he would say. Once, when walking across the pasture behind the Brockwood Grove, I was about to pass between a group of five tall pine trees. He caught me by the arm and said: *No, around them. We must not disturb them.* He maintained that the roots of trees have a sound that we no longer hear. On another such walk, returning along Morton's farmhouse, a storm began to brew. Soon there was thunder and lightning. I was worried, as we were in an exposed place, but he enjoyed the turmoil.

He used to say that when all of your senses are awake, then you are intelligent; when not all are awake, then thought arises. Whenever I walked with him I had the impression that he wasn't looking all around; he seemed to be looking straight ahead and walking rather fast. He nevertheless appeared to be completely

---

27 Scott Forbes joined Brockwood as a teacher in 1974 and went on to establish its video department. He headed the development of the Krishnamurti Centre at Brockwood, which he then helped to run with his wife, Kathy. He was principal of Brockwood Park School from 1985 to 1994 and continues to work in the field of holistic education. He is the editor of the memoirs of Mary Zimbalist, available freely online at inthepresenceofk.org

Below Brockwood Park

aware of everything, and he conveyed the feeling of that sensitivity to those who were with him.

Once when walking up from the lake at Buchillon, I picked a thyme flower for him to smell. The smell made him jump. In May 1983 during his first public talk at Ojai that year, he said: *If you lose relationship with nature, you lose relationship with man.* For me, K's relationship with nature and beauty can be summed up in the following two quotations.

The setting sun had transformed everything

Heaven was the earth and the earth heaven; the setting sun had transformed everything. The sky was blazing fire, bursting in every streak of cloud, in every stone, in every blade of grass, in every grain of sand. The sky was ablaze with green, purple, violet, indigo, with the fury of flame. Over that hill it was a vast sweep of purple and gold; over the southern hills a burning delicate green and fading blues; to the east there was a counter sunset as splendid in cardinal red and burnt ochre, magenta and fading violet. The counter sunset was exploding in splendour as in the west; a few clouds had gathered themselves around the setting sun and they were pure, smokeless fire which would never die. The vastness of this fire and its intensity penetrated everything and entered the earth. The earth was the heavens and the heavens the earth. And everything was alive and bursting with colour and colour was god, not the god of man.

Krishnamurti's Notebook
entry of 17 November 1961, Rishi Valley
© 1976 Krishnamurti Foundation Trust Ltd

Relationship with nature

If you establish a relationship with it [the tree], then you have a relationship with mankind. You are responsible then for that tree and for the trees of the world. But if you have no relationship with the living things on this earth, you may lose whatever relationship you have with humanity, with human beings. We never look deeply into the quality of a tree; we never really touch it, feel its solidity, its rough bark, and hear the sound that is part of the tree. Not the sound of wind through the leaves, not the breeze of a morning that flutters the leaves, but its own sound, the sound of the trunk and the silent sound of the roots. You must be extraordinarily sensitive to hear the sound. This sound is not the noise of the world, not the noise of the chattering of the mind, not the vulgarity of human quarrels and human warfare but sound as part of the universe.

It is odd that we have so little relationship with nature, with the insects and the leaping frog and the owl that hoots among the hills calling for its mate. We never seem to have a feeling for all living things on the earth. If we could establish a deep, abiding relationship with nature, we would never kill an animal for our appetite, we would never harm, vivisect, a monkey, a dog, a guinea pig for our benefit. We would find other ways to heal our wounds, heal our bodies. But the healing of the mind is something totally different. That healing gradually takes place if you are with nature, with that orange on the tree, and the blade of grass that pushes through the cement, and the hills covered, hidden, by the clouds.

This is not sentiment or romantic imagination but a reality of a relationship with everything that lives and moves on the earth. Man has killed millions of whales and is still killing them. All that we derive from their slaughter can be had through other means. But apparently man loves to kill things, the fleeting deer, the marvellous gazelle, and the great elephant. We love to kill each other. This killing of other human beings has never stopped throughout the history of man's life on this earth. If we could – and we must – establish a deep, long, abiding relationship with nature, with the actual trees, the bushes, the flowers, the grass and the fast-moving clouds, then we would never slaughter another human being for any reason whatsoever.

Krishnamurti to Himself
entry of 25 February 1983, Ojai, California
© 1987 Krishnamurti Foundation Trust Ltd

Something that happened in India might also indicate his intimate relationship with living things. On the path from Rajghat to Sarnath, which the Buddha was said to have walked, there was a plantation of large mango trees that had stopped yielding fruit. Even though it was said the Buddha had rested under these trees, there was a plan to remove them. K recounted how one day he'd walked among the trees and said to them: *Listen, if you do not bear any fruit, they are going to cut you down.* Asit Chandmal, too, records this story, in his book *One Thousand Suns*, finishing with K then saying: *They bore fruit that year. I am not saying it had anything to do with me.*

Once on a walk at Rishi Valley we passed several spathodea trees that had just been planted. They looked like bare trunks but when K went near and looked very closely he discovered a tiny bud on one of them. The next day there was a little leaf peeping out, which caused him much delight.

K enjoyed gardening, and particularly during his earlier days at Ojai he did a lot of it. When I showed him my garden at Buchillon, which I had set up myself, he remarked: *It's good to feel the earth between one's fingers.*

In the Grove at Brockwood Park, Hampshire, England

He once suggested that I visit the Grand Canyon and stay at the old hotel El Tovar, where he had stayed. I was finally able to do this in 1996. In 1923 K wrote: *... go to the Grand Canyon, in Arizona. If you have the eyes you will see the creator and the creation.*

Whenever I arrived at Brockwood from California, I'd feel tired for a time, due to the eight-hour time difference and the change in climate. On occasion I'd have a nap beneath a larch tree that stood in a clearing in the Grove, the sunshine warming me pleasantly. I told K about this and he responded: *Oh, I couldn't sleep out there. Too many things to see.* And he rolled his large eyes from right to left, as he did when doing his eye exercises.

During his last years, K continued to take walks at Brockwood, usually with a few friends. Dorothy Simmons would bring along her dog, and K enjoyed throwing sticks for him, something he could do with considerable energy even at the age of 89. Occasionally it was just K and me, and on one such walk there was a fence to be climbed. I was already on the other side, a little impatient, when the thought came, "He really needs quite some time to get over the fence." As if he had read my mind he replied: *I hope at my age you will climb over the fence this well.* I then asked him if he was afraid, to which he gave a strong *No*.

I have, I believe, experienced K's capacity to read thought, and other people have borne testimony to it themselves. Once, at Madras, K, several of his old friends and I were walking along Adyar Beach. On the way back I was behind K and happened silently to wonder what his friends might be thinking about his being so nice to this newcomer. Just then K turned round to me and said: *I don't think that way.*

A friend of mine once claimed that K would 'drop' me as he had 'dropped' others. I mentioned this to someone else who then told K, and the second friend reported back that K had become rather sad, saying: *I never dropped anybody, but people dropped me.*

Another incident occurred in the dining room at Brockwood. A journalist had just asked me what I did for a living. The question irked me and I was on the point of answering him, rather provocatively, that I did nothing, when K, who was sitting next to me, nipped in before me and said: *They make taps.*

In fact K had laughed during one of our first meetings at Brockwood when I told him that our company produced sanitary faucets. I was in my early 20s when, soon after the war, I started working in my father's factory. Manufacturing anything at that time was exceptionally difficult but most necessary, as Germany was all but destroyed and everything was needed. Needless to say, manufacturing products of export quality was a tremendous struggle. Yet within a few years our company had become the largest manufacturer in the world specializing in faucets. So when I told K what I had been doing I must have sounded peculiarly proud ... and of bathroom fixtures! That's when he laughed.

I also mentioned to him how difficult it had been to get the staff to cooperate with each other, and how much I had desired to have friendly relations with my colleagues in management. K replied: *Do you know how difficult it is to get people to cooperate?* Soon I was to discover that even within the Foundations people at that time found it difficult to work together.

Another time, at Rishi Valley, a professor (of Indian ancestry) from a South African university was sitting at our table. K was asking pointed questions concerning the situation in that country, trying in a variety of ways to get him to say what his personal feeling about it was, but our guest would answer only in generalities. Finally K, referring suddenly to me, said: *Mr. Grohe couldn't stand it in South Africa.* I was astonished. Admittedly, I had told him that I had worked there. I hadn't mentioned, however, that a year into my work I couldn't stand it any longer and returned to Europe, even though my parents were going to have a beautiful house in South Africa and were planning to live there for at least a few years. My father, fearing the Russians after the war, had relocated the family there from Germany. On one occasion I talked to K about the Germans' fear of the Russians. He said they had been right to be worried.

I once mentioned to K that I had had great problems with my father. He said: *Yes, you* had *problems* (with the emphasis on the "had"). Near the beginning of my time at Brockwood, he asked me: *What does your family think about the things you are doing here?* I hesitated, because I still had some hope, but he firmly interjected: *They're all against. It's always the same thing.* With time, I realized how right he was. Surprisingly, perhaps, my father, shortly before he died, did seem to see some sense in the little of K that he read, but added, "Oh, but that's difficult." Having asked many staff members and visitors to the Schools and Study Centres how they had come upon the teachings, it has become clear to me that unless the first contact, usually through a book, is felt by the person to be a revelation, he or she won't continue with it.

I once helped to organize an interview of K by a publisher from Czechoslovakia, Jadry Prokorny. Prokorny asked K what he would have done had he been living under a dictatorship. K answered that he would have been able to speak *only to friends, like you two.* In conversations and public talks K repeatedly pointed to the repression and brutality of dictatorships. He took an interest in everything, world politics included. He liked to watch political and news programmes on television and, even on his deathbed, enquired: *What's going on in the world?*

But he did not like to talk about war. One day K, Mary Zimbalist and I were driving from Brockwood to nearby Winchester. On the way we passed a huge, wide hollow among the fields, which Mary indicated was the place where Eisenhower had addressed the Allied troops before the invasion of Normandy.[28] K somewhat impatiently brushed aside the remark, saying: *The war has been over for a long time.* He was well aware of what had happened during World War II and often pointed out that the cruelty of that and other wars continued into the present. He once told me that when the British bombed Hamburg, they first targeted the centre so that the inhabitants would try to escape to the outskirts. Then they bombed the outskirts. He emphasized that nationalism is a common cause of division and conflict in the world. Often he said about himself: *I am not Indian.*

K once told us about an event that occurred in the 1930s. He was in Rome and visiting St. Peter's Square when the Pope was carried by in a sedan chair. The Pope stopped, leaned out and asked K, "Are you an Indian?" K replied: *I am supposed to be from India.* And the Pope said to him, "I like your face," after which he leaned back and continued on his way.

Although K sometimes mentioned that he had been brought up by English aristocracy, he would occasionally make reference to the *stuffy English society*. At one point he noticed my cuff links and told me that he and his brother had had cuff links and tie pins. They would leave them at home before going for a walk and once, at Ojai, they returned to find them gone – stolen. They were very happy they had disappeared.

Nevertheless, regarding Annie Besant – who was from England and whom he had loved like a mother – he said she had done more for India than Mahatma Gandhi. Using the example of Gandhi, he stated that any kind of forcing others to do what one wanted – even by the presumably peaceful means of fasting – was violent. Fasting for political reasons was violence.

---

28 The site is now famous also as a rock-concert venue.

K was a tremendously serious person but he also enjoyed a good laugh and took particular delight in telling good jokes. We shared many such moments. Here are three of the many jokes that he would sometimes recount:

Three sages in the Himalayas are sitting in silence, meditating. Ten years go by, and the first one says, "What a wonderful morning." Another ten years go by, and the second one says, "It might rain." Another ten years go by, and the third one says, "When will the two of you ever stop chattering!"

Saint Peter shows God what's happening on Earth. The first thing they see is a group of people labouring from morning till night. God is amazed and asks, "What is the matter with those people down there?" Saint Peter replies, "Didn't you say they had to earn their bread by the sweat of their brow?" God answers, "But I was only joking." Next they see robed cardinals and bishops at lavish tables piled with food and wine. And when God asks who those people are, Saint Peter tells Him, "They, my Lord, are the people who understood you were only joking."

A man is hanging from a cliff, shouting "Help! Help!", when a voice from above advises, "Have faith! Let go!" The man calls out, "Is nobody else up there?"

At some point at Brockwood, K read the Old Testament. When I asked him how he liked it, he answered: *I do like it. Not the tall tales* [he used the French word *blagues*] *they tell you, but the language, the style.* He also enjoyed reading detective stories as a pastime and appreciated a well-constructed plot.

K once asked: *When two egotists get married, what do you get?* After a brief, expectant silence from those present, he answered: *Just two egotists.* And during a question and answer meeting at Brockwood in 1984, he remarked about marriage: *When one has the time, the money and the energy, one can start the whole circus again.*

I felt he was referring to me, and felt strangely touched, because I was in the process of getting married a second time, in spite of K having told me *Good* when I mentioned at our first meeting in Gstaad that I was divorced. I knew he was fond of my fiancée and expected he would approve, but he just raised his arms and declared: *One marries, just like that.* On another occasion he said: *He marries the most beautiful woman, and has hell on earth.* He called Magda, my new wife, Madame A.G. At Brockwood he had suggested that I change my name to A.G. When I asked him what it meant, he explained *Ange Gardien (Guardian Angel)*.

I suppose that K and I got along rather well because I didn't want or expect anything from him. I didn't even know what to ask him, and in any case all of us could listen to what he had to say during innumerable public talks, dialogues and interviews. It is a huge body of work, and one can study it all one's life and still discover something new each day. This is partly because K would explore even often-repeated questions freshly each time, always approaching them from a different angle; and also because at each moment we can observe for ourselves human consciousness in action.

I remember when K and I once walked side by side in the corridor to the dining room. He took my hand and said with the intensity which he so frequently displayed: *I don't know why I like you so much. This has never happened to me before. It has nothing to do with the money – je m'en fiche (– I don't care at all).* On one occasion he told me: *We are brothers.* Several years later I asked Sunanda Patwardhan[29], an old friend of K's and a trustee of KFI, what he might have meant. She replied that K simply fell in love with people.

On 4 August 1928, at the Ommen Star Camp, K said to his audience: *I am in love, not with you, but with that which is behind you; not with your faces and your clothes, but with that which is life.*

---

29 See footnote 39 on page 62.

SAANEN, SCHÖNRIED
AND ROUGEMONT

During the 1984 Saanen talks K couldn't stay at Chalet Tannegg, as it was being sold, so a flat was rented for him at nearby Schönried. He showed us a number of pictures that hung in his bedroom there, of old ocean liners, on one of which he had sailed. He watched a few of the sprint competitions that were part of the Olympic Games that summer, shown on television, and called out to Mary Zimbalist: *Maria, look how they run! Look how they run!*

At one point he wondered why they hadn't gone to Spiez for a boat ride on Lake Thun the past few years. He corrected my German pronunciation, SHPEETS, to SHPEE-ets as the Swiss say it. Then he answered his own question: *Too much work to do.* Mary Zimbalist added, "We are getting too old."

Twice, my old school friend Edgar Hämmerle, from Austria, and I were invited for lunch at K's flat. Edgar had been living as a kind of sociable hermit in a wooden cabin without electricity, telephone or running water, taking care of various animals, including a big eagle owl. When K met Edgar for the first time he immediately asked him whether he was some kind of farmer, and they went on to have a lively conversation about animals and the like.

It was well known that K had a special relationship with animals. One day for lunch we went to the Klösterli Restaurant, near Gsteig, where especially good salads from their organic garden were served. The owner of the restaurant was very fond of dogs. While we were sitting at the table, his dog came and lay under K's chair. The owner was amazed and said he had never before seen his dog lie down under a guest's chair.

View towards Videmanette, in Rougemont

K enjoyed talking about his experiences with animals, but more than any other he loved telling the story of the tiger. In India some friends took him in a car to see a tiger in the wild. Eventually a tiger appeared and approached the car. K moved to stroke the animal but his companion quickly pulled his arm back. K was convinced that nothing detrimental would have happened to him. He was simply unafraid.[30]

Another story, which happened at Rajghat, concerns a monkey. One day as K was doing yoga exercises in his room, a large wild monkey jumped onto the window sill, stretching out his hand towards K. K grasped it, and so they sat there for a while, K and the monkey, holding hands.[31]

Once during lunch at Ojai, K told the story of how he had gone for a long walk there. On his way home he heard a barking dog. He pointed out that one could tell by the bark whether a dog was dangerous. This one evidently was. As there was no other way to get home, he had to pass by the house where the dog was. As he approached, the dog ran up to him and started circling him. Suddenly he grabbed K's arm between his jaws, whereupon K admonished him: *You go home!* And that, indeed, is what the dog did. He then explained how to handle vicious dogs according to what a French army officer had told him: hold a stick horizontally for the dog to dig his teeth into, then kick him in the belly. K did not appear to need this kind of defense, however, and he did not recommend it to us.

And a final story about animals: at one point while at Brockwood, in my room in the west wing, I suddenly woke up, turned on the light and found bats crowding the ceiling. I opened

---

30 You can read more about this in the October 2, 1973 entry in *Krishnamurti's Journal*.

31 K described this scene in the book *The Only Revolution*; it also appears in the *Penguin Second Krishnamurti Reader*, pp. 42–43.

the window further, turned off the light, and the next morning they were gone. But I always had the feeling that they had been attracted to the west wing because of K.

My friend Edgar was very fond of drinking a bit of wine. When he saw none at my house, he was quite disappointed, and naturally he did not expect that there would be any at Schönried when we went there for lunch. So he was pleasantly surprised to find a splendid bottle of red wine on the table. K immediately told him: *You can drink the whole bottle.* K, as a matter of course, did not have any.

But the conversation was very animated on both their parts. Knowing that Edgar and I had attended the same school at Davos, K asked him if I had gone to school mainly to learn or to ski. Edgar supposed that it was mainly to ski, and K made a facial expression as if to say he had expected as much.

At one point K mentioned to Edgar that some people in India came to his public talks even though they didn't understand English, because they wanted to be close to a saint. Edgar then stated that K was not a saint, and K replied: *Yes, but they think so.*

The second time we had lunch together, Edgar had planned to return home from Schönried by train. We were having an animated conversation when I asked, with some misgiving, when the train was due to depart. It turned out that there were only five minutes to get to the station, so everyone leapt up and I said to Edgar, "We have to run." "No, no," interjected Mary, "I'll drive you to the station in my car." She started upstairs to get the car keys. K raised his arms and shouted: *You have to run! You have to run!* Mary climbed even faster, while Edgar and I raced wildly downstairs, out of the house and to the station. The train was pulling in just as we arrived, panting heavily. The next time I met K, he said: *I watched how you ran.*

K was very observant, even with regard to small things. Once at Ojai when I dressed to go to lunch with him, I couldn't find

*K with Iris Soppa, the daughter of a friend of mine, before lunch
in Rougemont in 1985*   © Asit Chandmal

the belt for my trousers and went without one. There were several
other guests there, so it was two days later, on my return, that he
asked me casually: *Did you find your belt?* Another time I arrived
wearing an expensive imitation-leather jacket. K touched it and
asked: *Est ce que c'est de la peau? (Is it skin?)* He was amazed when
I told him it wasn't.

Nothing seemed to escape his notice. There was a time I was
having some chest pain, quite considerable, but I tried not to pay
it much attention, nor did I see a doctor. At one point, as I walked
past K, he lightly tapped my chest with his fingers. It was only
afterwards, when the pain disappeared, that I realized what he
had done. I later heard similar stories from others.

Another time I was having difficulty understanding a bank
statement for an account I had recently opened in Ojai. I asked

Mary, who was from the US, to explain it to me. As she was doing so, K approached and walked around us, saying: *Maria, be very attentive.* He kept repeating this until Mary responded, "But I am attentive." After a while, it appeared to me that nothing was more interesting than that boring bank statement.

Time and again K talked about total attention, but often after a public talk the audience seemed to be hypnotized. On those occasions, he would say: *Please don't be mesmerized. Please get up.*

In general, K spoke passionately but without pathos. I asked him once whether he prepared his talks. He answered: *No, for I wouldn't know what to say.*

Once, after a particularly impressive talk at Saanen in 1985, I went to see K in his apartment. He was stretched out on his bed, his doctor having advised him to rest after each talk. I told him that it had been wonderful. He became very serious and a great dignity emanated from him as he simply concurred: *C'etait merveilleux. (It was wonderful.)*

A woman from Italy who came for lunch one time reported that, at a conference of healers and clairvoyants, it had been stated that spiritual healing and clairvoyance do not work when thoughts interfere. K commented simply: *This is what we've been saying for the last seventy years.*

It was around this time that Pupul Jayakar[32], in Rougemont, told K that it was difficult to understand him. He resolutely

---

32 Pupul Jayakar (Pupulji) spent a lifetime in social work and was prominent in the Indian handicrafts industry. She was a close associate and confidante of Indira Gandhi, the Indian Prime Minister from 1966–84, and was her adviser on cultural matters. She met K in 1948 and was closely associated with him thereafter, becoming a trustee of KFI and authoring *Krishnamurti, A Biography*. A fine selection from the intense dialogues she had with K can be found in the book *Fire in the Mind*. She died in 1997.

replied: *I must become simpler.* And, in fact, on the following days he expressed himself even more simply and clearly.

During the 1985 public talks, K stayed at Rougemont. I placed my rented apartment at Chalet l'O Perrevoué at his disposal, and KFT rented an additional large flat in the same chalet to accommodate some helpers and companions, in this case Michael, Raman and Dr. Parchure, as well as possible guests such as Vanda Scaravelli[33]. The previous year we had invited K for lunch there, and he had greatly admired the dining table with its heavy and well-made wooden top. He was generally very aware and highly appreciative of quality in things.

After some time, K moved from the lower apartment to the one on the upper floor, because it was more spacious and had a balcony. He was also glad that, by doing so, Mary Zimbalist no longer had to share a bathroom. He remarked chivalrously: *You know, she is a lady.* Another time, when the three of us were taking the car, I tried to help K into it although he didn't really need help. Mary was coming from the other side and, pointing to her, he said: *She is a lady,* which made me rush to help her.

Around that time K deeply burned his finger on a brass reading lamp. I was horrified when I saw the wound, but K dismissed it, saying: *Oh, I can stand lots of pain.*

His daily walk during this time was a stroll along the Saane/Sarine River, beside the airfield in Saanen. He was too weak to do more. He told me: *You can come with us, but for you it would be nothing.*

---

33 Vanda Scaravelli met K in 1937. K became close friends with her and her husband and often visited them at their large villa in Fiesole, near Florence. She rented Chalet Tannegg in Gstaad for K during the Saanen Gatherings. A yoga enthusiast, she wrote a well regarded book on the subject, *Awakening the Spine.* She died in 1999 at the age of 91.

One day the actor Richard Gere came for lunch. Although K had already given a public talk that day, he conversed very intensely with him for more than an hour. It was almost as though K was giving another talk, and we left the lunch table at 4 o'clock. When he was on the point of leaving, Richard Gere, who appeared visibly moved, asked K if he could give him a hug. It was quite touching to see this much taller man bend down and embrace K so that K's slight figure almost disappeared in the other's arms.

It was also in Rougemont that my elder son, Christoph, who is now a vintage-car dealer, showed K his first meticulously restored old MG. K showed a great deal of interest and looked under the hood in his usual careful way. Christoph, tongue in cheek, proclaimed, "It's now a holy car."

I also wanted to bring my younger son, John, to lunch. When we finally settled on a date, I happily relayed the information to K, who replied: *But he will be bored.* Realizing how true this was, as John was a teenager at the time, I cancelled right away, to my son's great relief. Even so, both John and Christoph had been to Ojai and met K at lunches there, and both had been to public talks either at Ojai or Saanen. Christoph had even visited Rishi Valley with me.

At some point, K recounted several stories about women who kept following him around. At Madras a woman had invaded his bathroom by climbing through the window and he had had to call for help. Another woman had beseeched him to let her touch his foot. When at last he acquiesced she grabbed his ankle and wouldn't let go. He laughed until there were tears in his eyes and concluded with: *We are all crazy, but they beat us!* He enjoyed telling anecdotes, liked to laugh and really appreciated good jokes.

K was fond of the French language and in the last year of his life asked Mary Zimbalist to organize French lessons for him in Santa Barbara. Unfortunately, he never had a chance to proceed with them. Once during lunch he was telling us about Paris, where he had spent quite a bit of time particularly during the 1920s. He knew a maharaja then who collected cars and would buy any model he did not yet own, and K accompanied him for such purchases. K told the story of the car dealers who simply refused to believe that it was not K who was the maharaja. When I remarked that Paris was no longer what it had been, K responded: *Vous savez … (You know …)*, in a tone implying that it still had something.

During this last year of Saanen talks, I started building a new chalet. K was very curious to know where it would be and why I was building it, so I described the location and told him that I had always wanted a wooden house. Sometime later, either at lunch or during a public talk, he said: *To build your own house is still self-centredness.*

Another time he commented with some admiration on the orderly way in which the Swiss stack their firewood. He speculated as to what Americans might feel about that kind of activity: *Ah, we have no time for something like this; life is too short.*

With K staying in Rougemont, I asked the woman who had been cleaning for me for four years (and who continues to do so after thirty years) to attend also to K. She would enter his apartment while he was having breakfast, and he always stood up to greet her. When it came time for him to leave Rougemont, she bid him goodbye: "Au revoir, Monsieur Krishnamurti. A l'année prochaine." ("Until next year.") To which K replied: *Si dieu veut. (God willing.)*

LAST JOURNEYS TO INDIA

In November 1985, at Rajghat, K told me that he still had some months to live. When I reminded him that he had promised us he would live another ten years, he only raised his arms as if to say, What can one do?

K's health had started to deteriorate at Brockwood. The regular walks that he took became shorter. The walk through the Grove and across the pastures and fields, which entailed climbing over a fence, he did not do anymore. Apart from that, he was as active as ever. Once he told me: *Je travaille comme un fou! (I am working like mad!)*

Indifference and understanding

One has to be indifferent – to health, to loneliness, to what people say or do not say, indifferent to whether one succeeds or does not succeed, indifferent to authority. If you hear somebody shooting, making a lot of noise with a gun, you can very easily get used to it, and you turn a deaf ear; that is not indifference. Indifference comes into being when you listen to that noise with no resistance, go with that noise, ride on that noise infinitely. Then that noise does not affect you, does not pervert you. Then you listen to every noise in the world – the noise of your children, of your wife, of the birds, the noise of the chatter the politicians make. You listen to it completely with indifference and therefore with understanding.

On Living and Dying, pg. 99
6th talk, Bombay, 7 March 1962
© 1992 Krishnamurti Foundation Trust Ltd
and Krishnamurti Foundation of America

K had been very enthusiastic when he said to me at Brockwood in 1984: *You come with us to India.* How could one resist? He invited me to live close to where he lived and, for health reasons, to eat the same food. *You stay with us!* he said when I was to go to Rishi Valley, Rajghat and Madras for the first time.[34] Later that year, in Schönried, he asked me to live with him. I knew what that meant: to drop everything, and I was not ready for it.

Now, in the autumn of 1985, I was travelling with K on his last journey to India.

It was an early morning departure from Brockwood. The day had not yet dawned, yet all the staff and students, about one hundred people, had come to the west wing and were waiting at the bottom of the staircase to see us off. K shook hands on his way to the door. The atmosphere was solemn. A premonition hung in the air that this might have been K's last visit.

Dorothy Simmons, the former principal of the School, drove us to the airport in her car. K and I sat in the back, with Mary Zimbalist in the front. At the start there was rain, but it soon stopped, and Dorothy forgot to turn off the wipers. They began to scrape across the dry windscreen. I became tense and would have liked to say something but instead waited for a reaction from K. And, as so often happened, his response was not what I would have said. It was simply *It's stopped raining,* and Dorothy immediately turned them off.

At the airport the moment of parting brought tears to the eyes of the women. Dorothy and Mary were staying behind, I was the only one flying with K. Rita Zampese[35], Lufthansa's public rela-

---

34 It was during this, my first time in India, that K and Pupul Jayakar invited me to be a trustee of KFI.

35 Rita Zampese is a long-time friend of Brockwood. She took the photographs of K and me at Rishi Valley that appear on pg. 63 and the back page, and she continues to visit Rishi Valley every year.

tions manager in London, led us through to the lounge.[36] We found ourselves sitting near a group of men and women, business people probably, who appeared very self-absorbed. They were talking loudly, smoking and drinking alcohol. K looked at them with wide eyes, and the expression on his face was one of astonishment and mild horror, although he was not the least bit contemptuous.

We had to change at Frankfurt, and I remember with what joy K travelled on the fast electric shuttle between terminals. On the larger plane, he had the single seat at the front and to the right, which only Lufthansa was able to offer. By contrast, I found myself sitting by a gentleman who was reading a newspaper and listening to music at the same time. What's more, he made hand movements as a conductor might. He, too, was self-engrossed and showed not the slightest interest in his neighbours – in this case, K and me. It was night-time when we flew over Russia and Afghanistan. On the plane K said: *I'm glad we two are alone.*

After arriving at Delhi, K went with Pupul Jayakar to stay at her house. I went to a hotel, where I was the only European but also the only one wearing Indian clothes. Every day at sunset we met at Lodi Park. It was always at sunset, because K had once suffered from sunstroke and had to keep out of the strongest rays. At the entrance there was a kind of turnstile, which glistened with the sweat and dirt of many hands. I would open it with my foot, and K would exclaim *Good!*

The park was well kept, with many trees, lawns, waterways and bridges, and buildings from pre-Mogul times. At dusk innumer-

---

36 My entire luggage consisted of one rucksack, which I took with me onto the aircraft. Now I cannot imagine how I could have set off on such a journey with so few things.

able birds would gather and settle down for the night. The noise they made was deafening. Occasionally Nandini Mehta[37] or Radhika Herzberger's[38] daughter, Maya, would join us on our walks, as would Pama Patwardhan[39].

One man in Lodi Park recognized him and approached rather aggressively, demanding, "Are you Krishnamurti? You should stay in India! Here are your roots!" K replied: *I am nobody.* Then he raised his open hands to me and said: *You see, they have a fixed idea and stick to it.* Despite such incidents, K was friendly towards everyone he met and especially so towards the poor and those who were normally ignored by others, such as the ice-cream vendor at the entrance to the park.

K once mentioned that many years earlier he'd been asked by several followers of Gandhi what he thought about the caste system in India not allowing certain people into the temples. He

---

37 Nandini Mehta was Pupul Jayakar's sister. She met K in 1947 and became a close friend. It was she to whom K wrote the letters that can be found in Pupul Jayakar's biography of K, in the chapter Happy Is the Man Who Is Nothing, which KFT has republished as *Letters to a Young Friend*. She founded the Bal Anand School for underprivileged children in Bombay and was a trustee of KFI. She died in 2002.

38 Radhika Herzberger, Pupul Jayakar's daughter, had known K from childhood. She is director of Rishi Valley Education Centre and a trustee of KFI. In 2013 she was awarded the Padma Shri Award for literature and education by the government of India.

39 Pama Patwardhan, along with his wife, Sunanda (author of *A Vision of the Sacred – My Personal Journey with Krishnamurti*), and his brother Achyut (formerly a famous freedom fighter in India), became close associates of K in 1947. All three were trustees of KFI. Achyut remained a bachelor all his life, and I once asked him how he had 'escaped'. He replied that he had not escaped; rather, his affair of the heart had not ended as he had wished and he had not been moved in the same way again. Achyut died in 1992, Sunanda in 1999 and Pama in 2007.

With K at Rishi Valley, end 1984/beginning 1985 © Rita Zampese

replied: *It doesn't matter who goes in, because god isn't there.* He spoke about this in 1975:

An idea put together by thought

Without compassion, which means passion for everything, care for everything, respect for everything, without compassion what is sacred can never be found. You understand? You know we have created – thought has created something sacred – the temples, the churches, the symbols – and we worship those symbols, and call those sacred. But it is the movement of thought in time and measure. So that is not sacred. Once in India, the speaker was asked by the followers of Mr Gandhi, who said, "All peoples can enter, every type of strata of human society can enter into that temple, for god is there for everyone." And they asked me, "What do you say to that question?" I said, "Anybody can enter, it doesn't matter who goes in, because god isn't there." You understand? God is an idea put together by thought. But one has to find that which is eternally, incorruptibly sacred. And that can only come when there is compassion, which means when you have understood the whole significance of suffering – suffering not only of yourself, but the suffering of the world.

5th public dialogue, Saanen, 3 August 1975
© Krishnamurti Foundation Trust Ltd

When I mentioned this quote to an old friend, she told me another such story: A beggar is crying in front of a temple, and God comes along and asks him why. The beggar says, "They won't let me in the temple," and God replies, "Me neither."

Travelling, and the frequent change of climate it entailed, exhausted K, and his health deteriorated in Delhi. He did not sleep well and he ate very little. He used to say that he would have become much older if he hadn't had to travel so much. He once told us that many years earlier he had travelled by train from New York to California, taking three days and nights. I asked him if this was tiring, and he said: *Yes, very much.*

From Delhi I went on my own to the Krishnamurti Retreat Centre near Uttarkashi in the Himalayas. A school would be established there some years later, but it was closed after the people responsible for it encountered difficulties. In any case, K hadn't wanted to have a school there but rather a retreat centre.

After I'd made the long Dehradun to New Delhi return trip by taxi, I mentioned to K my feeling that in India the countryside is paradise and the cities are hell. He agreed.

Drivers in India tend to blow their car horns constantly, alerting the many pedestrians to their presence. I'd finally told my taxi driver that I'd give him 100 rupees if he didn't blow his horn, and that worked very well. The pedestrians became much more attentive!

On the plane to Varanasi, K kept the window shade down because of the bright sun. But time and again he would open it to look at the white peaks of the Himalayas. We agreed that the mountains were really something!

He told me that once, as a young man, he had been clambering around the Zugspitze, in Germany, in casual shoes. A mountain guide who passed by with a group of alpinists on a rope noticed K. After scolding him, the guide tied him to the end of the rope and led him down the mountain. K told me he had not been afraid and could have descended safely by himself.

I was overwhelmed with the atmosphere at Rajghat in Varanasi. Here one can especially sense the enchantment that appears to exist in all of the places where K lived. It can be felt at Brockwood, Rishi Valley, Vasanta Vihar – K's home in Madras and the headquarters of KFI – and Ojai. One could also find it at Chalet Tannegg in Gstaad and both Pupulji's government house in Delhi, which was full of ancient sculptures and other works of art, and her apartment in Bombay. The surroundings in all of these places are strikingly beautiful and immaculately kept: islands of serenity amidst the turmoil of the world, full of trees, flowers, birds and butterflies; there is a kind of sacredness about them.

Walking around the grounds of the School at Rajghat, one comes upon several archaeological excavation sites. The campus is situated in one of the most ancient parts of Varanasi, called Kashi, and presumably there were temples, parks and royal palaces there 4,000 to 5,000 years ago. Beyond the excavation sites a canal carries sewage from the city into the Ganges. The stench was noticeable all the way to the house where K was living. He laughed when Pupulji assured him that a new sewage system would be built in the near future. Apparently this promise had been made many times, and when I visited the following year nothing had yet been done. It was only during my visit at the end of 1988 that I noticed that construction of the huge new canal system had begun.

At Rajghat my room was underneath K's. As soon as he arrived he began intensive dialogues (see pg. 68). At sunset he would walk several times around the School's large sports field, accompanied by friends, whom he jokingly called his bodyguards. Even during these recreational walks he continued his discussions with them. His legs were becoming very weak, however, as he himself said, and after one walk he fell forward on the steps. His companions wanted to help him up but he refused to let them, saying: *If I fall on the steps that is my affair!*

When K could no longer walk quickly, I would go on my own, circling as briskly as I could. After such walks he would ask me how many rounds I had done and how long I had taken. When I told him that I had broken my record, he responded enthusiastically. Somebody must have complained to him, though, about this crazy guy chasing around the sports field, because he said in a meeting with friends: *He just wants to keep his body fit. What's wrong with that?*

It was customary to invite people for lunch with whom K would hold intense conversations. At Ojai and Saanen he would sometimes converse until 4 o'clock, even when he had given a public talk that morning. He liked to question those invited about their areas of specialization. Thus he was well informed about current developments in many fields, including politics, education, medicine, science and computers. Once the vice-chancellor of a uni-

Cave Rock in Rishi Valley

versity and his wife were invited to have lunch at Rajghat. K noted sadly that the man never once smiled at his wife, nor even looked at her.

Every once in a while, Vikram Parchure's[40] wife, Ambika, would bring along her lovely 3-year-old daughter. K would say to the little girl: *Don't forget that I want to be your first boyfriend.*

During the time that we were at Rajghat, a great many religious festivals were celebrated which were often very noisy. The temple next door would resound with fireworks, drums and singing late into the night. At 4 o'clock the next morning the

---

40 Vikram Parchure, one of Dr. Parchure's sons, taught at Rishi Valley School and helped to develop their rural women's programme. He assists KFI with their publications programme and has developed a series of 24 poster panels of K quotes and photographs from renowned photographers, called Crisis in the World, which has been translated into several languages and is displayed at gatherings and book fairs. He is also a trustee of the Quest Foundation in Thailand.

celebration would start up again. There was also an adjoining mosque from which we could hear the greatly amplified sing-song of the muezzin during our walks. None of this seemed to disturb K. If the muezzin had not yet started his calling and noticed K approaching, he would walk up to the fence to shake K's hands affectionately.

At this time, part of the Indian film *The Seer Who Walks Alone*, a documentary about K, was being shot at Rajghat. K had told the director: *I'll do anything you want me to do.* One scene shows K standing on a hill above the Varuna River, outlined against the setting sun like an ancient sculpture. He walks over the narrow bridge across the river and along the path to Sarnath, where the Buddha was said to have walked.

K was once with Donald Ingram Smith[41] in Sri Lanka, a pre-dominantly Buddhist country, and said: *If you listened to the Buddha, you wouldn't need Buddhism.*

When the time for his public talks drew near, K seemed to gain new energy. He gave three talks and held one question and answer meeting at Rajghat despite obvious signs of physical weakness. He also had three dialogues with Panditji[42] in the presence of thirty or forty others in the upper story of his house,

---

41 Donald Ingram Smith was a renowned writer-producer of radio programmes for the Australian Broadcasting Commission when he set sail for Sri Lanka in 1949 to hear K speaking there. He ended up recording him for Radio Lanka and accompanying him during his stay in the country. He is the author of *The Transparent Mind: My Journey with Krishnamurti*. He died in 2006 at 94.

42 Panditji, actually Pandit Jagannath Upadhyaya. Pandit (also pundit), a Sanskrit word meaning 'learned man', is the title of a person learned in Sanskrit and Hindu law, religion and philosophy, sometimes other subjects. Panditji was an eminent Buddhist and Hindu scholar with whom K enjoyed speaking. He died shortly after K, and their Indian friends said, "K wanted to have a chat with him."

which are recorded in the book *The Future Is Now* (also titled *The Last Talks*).[43] Kabir Jaithirtha[44] has told me that Panditji once asked K to put the teachings in one sentence. K replied: *Where the self is, there is no love; where there is love, there is no self.*

During these talks, one participant stood out through the clear and simple manner with which he communicated with K. At the time, I didn't know that this was P. Krishna[45], the new school director. K, despite poor health, was concerned with every aspect of the appointment of the director and gave all his time and energy to the matter. He invited Krishna and his family to lunch and talked affectionately with his wife and children; the grandfather came along once as well. As usual, K was interested in the practical details too, like the appropriate salary for the new director and that he had the use of a car. He felt enthusiastic about Krishna who, as a well-known physicist, had worked in the USA and Europe. He told me that when he had asked Krishna if

---

43 One of the participants was Samdhong Rinpoche (Lobsang Tenzin), a trustee of KFI. For many years he headed schools of Tibetan studies and was a member of the Assembly of Tibetan People's Deputies, appointed by the Dalai Lama. From 2001 to 2011 he was Prime Minister of the Tibetan government-in-exile, based in Dharamsala, India. He travels extensively on behalf of the cause of Tibetan autonomy. An interview with him appears in the book *Krishnamurti: 100 Years*.

44 Kabir Jaithirtha was principal of The Valley School, the K School in Bangalore. After K's death, he left to co-found, to the west of Bangalore, the K-inspired school Centre for Learning (CFL). More recently he helped to found another K-inspired school, to the south of Bangalore: Shibumi. He is a trustee of KFI.

45 P. Krishna, a cousin of Radha Burnier, had met K in 1958. He was Professor of Physics at Benares Hindu University when K made him head of Rajghat Education Centre. He is currently in charge of the study centre at the Rajghat Education Centre and a trustee of KFI. He travels within India and abroad to give talks on Krishnamurti, religion and science.

he would take over the School, Krishna deliberated and then announced, "I would be delighted." This was very fortunate, as there were then quite a few difficulties there.

Once we were sitting together with Krishna's lovely teenage daughters, and K told me in French: *Do you see how different they are?* Then he said to the others: *I'll translate. I said, You should not marry while you are too young.*

Finally, it was arranged that K would take his meals in bed, as he had hardly any chance to eat during these lunchtime conversations. He had told me once that he never had the sensation of hunger, though he could eat properly nevertheless. But these days, being unwell, he ate very little indeed.

After a walk one evening K asked R. R. Upasani[46], who intended to retire from the Agricultural College at Rajghat, where he was principal, if he would stay on to work for the Foundation. Upasani agreed to continue as long as K was there. I said to K, "Upasani should stay on even when you are not here." K immediately asked Upasani: *Sir, stay another year or more.* Upasani was so moved that he wept. It was getting dark, and suddenly K asked: *Where is he?* as he could not discern Upasani in the darkness. It marked the onset of a kind of night blindness.[47]

While he was at Rajghat, K several times addressed the subject of sex. He pointed out that of course we would not exist if it were not for sex, which was simply a part of life. Somebody

---

46 R. R. Upasani took up the position of Secretary of KFI in 1987. He established the retreat centre at Uttarkashi and the Nachiket School there, and he was Secretary of the Executive Committee for Sahyadri School, a K School begun after K's death. He died in 2008.

47 A decade later Upasani told me about something he had felt during one of K's last public talks, in India. He'd had the feeling that someone was going to shoot K. When he later mentioned this to K, K said yes and that it had taken all of his energy to prevent it.

Sunrise over the Ganges, at Rajghat

Fishermen off Adyar Beach, Madras (Chennai)

told K about a cross-cultural wedding where the guests were already gathered when it was discovered that the bridegroom had disappeared without explanation. K often referred to this story, wondering at the girl's apparent determination to marry despite the great difficulties inherent in such circumstances. At one point he wondered aloud: *Did they have sex?* The innocence of this remark caused considerable laughter among those present.

There are two other, rather random memories that I have regarding K at Rajghat. When he sat with several Theosophists in Annie Besant's old room on the campus, he asked them: *What shall we talk about?* Then he went on: *Oh yes, I'll tell you a few jokes.* Also, Annie Besant's coffee service was still in the room, but K did not have any recollection of it nor of the room itself. That coffee service must have been there for over sixty years.

After the public talks we flew via Delhi to Madras. At the time of our arrival the weather was pleasantly warm. The palm trees and flowering shrubs moved gently in the fresh breeze. As we drove, in a cabriolet, from the airport to Vasanta Vihar, I suddenly felt as if I was returning home. At that very moment K remarked: *It is like coming home!*

Later as we walked along the beach we witnessed the surf crashing thunderously onto the luminous yellow sand. There was a strong wind blowing but delicately-violet clouds hung in the sky. Against this background the full moon rose from the ocean just as the spectacular sun set opposite, which was mirrored for us on the surface of the Adyar River.

A few years ago while walking along Adyar Beach, I met a fisherman named Karuna Karan. He spoke English quite well, as he had studied for a time at the Theosophical Society's Olcott School. He told me that when he was a shy little boy, K had once grasped his hand and taken him for a fast walk. He claimed that almost no one could keep up with K. He also said that some villagers had asked K to look in on someone who was ill, and when he entered the person's hut their fever disappeared.

At one point at Madras in 1985, I went to his room and he was looking at a newly published book whose cover image was a photograph of himself. Somewhat amused, he pointed to the cover and remarked: *He looks a bit sad.*

After only a few days in Madras we left for Rishi Valley. We started out early and this time saw the sun rising as the moon simultaneously set in the west. We were travelling in a new car that was decidedly more comfortable than the old American one we had used on previous occasions. As usual, the car had been made available by a good friend, T. S. Santhanam[48]. We didn't stop until we had covered half the distance and the first hills were coming into view. The morning landscape was immensely peaceful. A motorcyclist, stopped beside the road, was amazed to see K there. K was no less astonished that someone should recognize him in this isolated spot.

K conversed with our friendly chauffeur about his family and insisted that he should send his children to Rishi Valley School. Later the man's son did indeed study there.

Radhika lived on the same floor as K at Rishi Valley. She and I would have breakfast in K's dining room. Sometimes, when he was feeling stronger, I would go to see him in his bedroom to say good morning. One time I said to him, regarding Rishi Valley, "It's almost nicer than Ojai, though it is similar." To which he replied: *Of course.*

Because he was feeling so weak his daily walks were often cancelled, but he still had a number of meetings with students

---

48 T. S. Santhanam was a businessman from Madras. His wife, Padma, was a trustee of KFI and very active at The School-KFI-Chennai. They died in 2005 and 2006, respectively. Their son, Viji, has been a member of KFI's Chennai Executive Committee for many years.

and teachers. During our last walk together at Rishi Valley, in December 1985, something happened. While I was looking with admiration at the lovely blue mountains east of the valley, K suddenly put his arm around my shoulder and said something like: *My dear friend.* Radhika was with us, and when she reminded me of the scene, I asked her to write it down:

> "As a party of us walked down the road, I could sense that he was straining every nerve to keep up with the small group of younger friends that walked with him that afternoon. But at one point, when we had reached the cluster of rocks under what the Rishi Valley children call Uday rock, his demeanor changed. There was an unexpected lull and I turned around to see the tension and effort go out of Krishnaji; he was his still and contemplative self. A moment later he turned around and embraced Friedrich, calling him *my friend.* Later that evening in his bedroom, saying goodnight to him, I said, 'Something happened to you this evening, didn't it?' Wearing the hooded look that came over him when he was approaching mystery, he said: *Good for you to have noticed.*"

Radhika's use of the term "hooded look" reminds me of an occasion in the crowded dining room at Vasanta Vihar when I was sitting across from K and he suddenly caught my eye. How can I describe the flame that came from him? It was like a volcano bursting. The whole person was on fire. It reminded me of the sunset at Rishi Valley that K had described: *You were of that light, burning, furious, exploding, without shadow, without root and word.*[49] I couldn't stand this force, so eventually looked down. None of the other guests seemed to have noticed.

---

49 See pg. 40 for more of this quotation from *Krishnamurti's Notebook.*

Windmill Rock in Rishi Valley. On a walk, K asked me: Who put those rocks there?

A similar thing happened at the table in the west wing kitchen at Brockwood in the presence of two other people. It was unlimited energy, an immense force that he emanated. Did he want to show us something? It seemed to express *Wake up* or *Come over.* It had urgency. He used to tell us *Move! Move!* Occasionally on our walks he would push me on the shoulder, which seemed to indicate the same thing. This reminds me of a walk at Brockwood when K was rising after tightening his shoes and I told him that my grandmother used to say at the end of a break, "Debout les Morts!" ("Rise, you dead people!") This he enjoyed very much.

I would sometimes try to observe K to guess what he was thinking. But I couldn't see anything; he was impenetrable. Perhaps because he wasn't thinking. David Moody writes in his book *The Unconditioned Mind:*

> "The conversation was coming to a close, and I gazed rather deeply into Krishnamurti's eyes. He met my gaze completely, without any undue sense of modesty or confrontation. As I looked into his eyes, I had the uncanny sense that there was no one present, no structure of identity, on the other side. Whether this was a projection or a valid intuition I cannot say. I felt he was observing me as completely as I was observing him, and yet at the same time it was like looking through a clear window, with only open space on the other side."[50]

After teachers from Brockwood, Ojai and the other Indian Schools arrived at Rishi Valley for an International Teachers Conference, it turned out that K was able to attend some of the

---

50 David Edmund Moody, *The Unconditioned Mind – J. Krishnamurti and the Oak Grove School*, pg. 55. © 2011. This material was reproduced by permission of Quest Books, the imprint of The Theosophical Publishing House (www.questbooks.net).

meetings. Because of his poor health, his active participation had not been planned, but it raised the discussions to a higher level. These talks, too, are included in the book *The Future Is Now/ The Last Talks.*

During his final two years visiting Rishi Valley, K spoke with the lovely younger pupils there, discussions that are available as MP3 recordings and on DVD. After one of the final discussions, K asked me: *Did you see these boys and girls? They will be thrown to the wolves.* His relationship with students and his views on education always fascinated me. The following gives an indication of how he saw education for young children.

Education for the very young

With the very young what is most important is to help them to free themselves from psychological pressures and problems. Now the very young are being taught complicated intellectual problems; their studies are becoming more and more technical; they are given more and more abstract information; various forms of knowledge are being imposed on their brains, thus conditioning them right from childhood. Whereas what we are concerned with is to help the very young to have no psychological problems, to be free of fear, anxiety, cruelty, to have care, generosity and affection. This is far more important than the imposition of knowledge on their young minds. This does not mean the child should not learn to read, write and so on, but the emphasis is on psychological freedom instead of the acquisition of knowledge, though that is necessary.

Letters to the Schools
now titled *The Whole Movement of Life Is Learning*
letter of 1 October 1979
© 1981 & 2006 Krishnamurti Foundation Trust Ltd

On one occasion at Rishi Valley we were talking with K about setting up an adult study centre. Suddenly a hoopoe bird came to the window and began pecking vigorously on the glass, obviously wanting to come in. K calmed it: *All right, all right, I'm here, I'm here.* Later Radhika told me that K often talked with the bird. She once entered his room and thought he must have a visitor, as he was saying: *You are welcome to bring your children, but they probably would not like it here because when I am gone they will shut the windows and you will not be able to find a way out.* Also regarding birds, it seems to me that it was Mary Cadogan who once told me that when K heard one of the first audio recordings of himself speaking to an audience in the open air in India, his response was: *Play it again, play it again – it was just like that!* When asked *what* was like that, he responded: *The birds! The birds!*

Another recollection of that visit to Rishi Valley is the time that a farmer driving a bullock cart invited me to jump up onto the back of it. It was a hard ride and I was gripping the side tenaciously. I was afraid that if the bullock took off I would go flying. We rode by K's room in the old guest house, and I looked for him at his window. He didn't seem to be there but later he said: *You were really holding tightly to the bullock cart.* I imagined him seeing me with a sixth sense, and others since then have told me similar stories.

On one walk at Rishi Valley, there was a beggar on the side of the road. K recognized him and shook his hand. Sometimes when villagers were walking towards us they would step off the road; K would try to get them back on. He was always concerned for poor people, and in a talk with students at Rishi Valley he described the long distances the village children had to walk to their school. He urged the Rishi Valley students to put pressure on their teachers to provide a bus for these children. To avoid this, one of the students said something like, "But you are the president, you could do something!" which caused some laughter. In 1984 at an International Trustees Meeting at Brockwood, K took Radhika's hand and made her promise to establish so-called satellite schools in the villages. She did so, and there are now nineteen of them.

The state of K's health made it difficult for me to fathom how he could possibly give the scheduled series of talks to thousands of people in Bombay. I felt great relief when he had them cancelled. After he returned to Madras, I travelled with a few teachers from Brockwood and Ojai to visit The Valley School in Bangalore. Afterwards I myself returned to Madras for another week and joined K on some of his walks along Adyar Beach.

On one of my last ever walks with K, on the beach, we had just reached the house of Radha Burnier when suddenly he took my arm firmly under his and we walked at high speed around the house. I wondered if he was exorcising it.

Soon K decided to leave for Ojai. It would be easier to obtain medical treatment while staying at Pine Cottage, and he would have more tranquillity there. Scott Forbes, who had travelled with him from Rishi Valley to Madras, was the perfect person to accompany him on this journey across the Pacific.

After returning to Europe, I spent three weeks in the Swiss mountains and then flew directly to California, for Ojai.

At the entrance to Pine Cottage, Ojai

… Someone comes along and is extraordinarily curious to know how a person like K lives.

Although K did not address these words to me, I felt that they could well apply to me. It was not so much his life story that I was interested in (how Theosophists discovered a neglected boy who then developed into the World Teacher) but rather how this extraordinary person who inspired such respect actually lived his daily life. As it turned out, my curiosity was more than satisfied.

In February 1986, at the age of 90, Krishnamurti, at the end of an extraordinary life, came back to Ojai to die.

While on his deathbed, mail came to him from around the world and he had it read to him. I was amazed at the banal and trivial things with which the dying man was presented.

Some months earlier K had told me he would soon die, and he had said the same to Erna Lilliefelt. Everyone was hoping for a recovery. Indeed, forty years before, at Ojai, he had once been so ill that his doctors had all but given up on him; yet a homeopathic doctor named Keller looked after him devotedly, for a whole year, and of course he did recover.[51]

---

51 This information was given to me in Ojai by Mrs. Keller.

A very moving account of K's death is given by Dr. Deutsch, his doctor at the time, in Evelyne Blau's[52] book *Krishnamurti: 100 Years*. Right till the end he was concerned about humanity and those who had come close to him – in other words, about others above all.

During these last days, Rukmini, a student at Oak Grove, wrote him a letter asking, as far as I can recall, "What will happen to the world once you are gone?" K had it read to him and, despite being in great pain and feeling very weak physically, he did not forget the matter, later asking at least twice whether his thanks had been conveyed. He left Rukmini a book (*Les Fables de La Fontaine*), which she has told me she enjoyed very much, and a string of Indian prayer beads.

And he could still laugh. When he enquired about my house in Ojai and I told him that construction was still going on and that it was hell, he laughed so hard I was afraid the feeding tubes that passed through his nose might move and cause him some pain.

But by now K was very ill, and he had asked for some of the trustees to come and be with him so that they could talk over urgent Foundation matters. In spite of terrible weakness and pain he spoke in his usual simple, clear way to these friends who had gathered from around the world.[53] He laid the responsibility

---

52 Evelyne Blau is a trustee of KFA. In addition to *Krishnamurti: 100 Years* (which includes the important 'dissolution of the Order of the Star' talk, as well as many people's recollections of K), she has edited, along with Mark Edwards, *All the Marvelous Earth* and has made several theme videos, as well as the films on K's life and teachings *With a Silent Mind* and *The Challenge of Change,* made with Michael Mendizza.

53 An account of K's last days can be found in the third volume, *The Open Door,* of Mary Lutyens's biography of K, as well as in the same author's *The Life and Death of Krishnamurti.*

The Nandi, a traditional Indian sculpture of a kneeling cow, near the Pepper Tree at Pine Cottage. One time, I saw it with flowers on its head and asked Mary Zimbalist if Indians had been visiting. She said K had told her to put flowers on it sometimes, so that it feels at home.

of cooperation on them. He said that the president and Secretary of the Foundations should not take on any other work. He talked about the possibility of bringing together a group of people whose main task would be to travel and *hold the whole thing together.*

He once told me at Brockwood while we were coming back from a walk: *This place should always stay like this*; and when he was asked what we ought to do after his death, he answered: *Care for the land and keep the teachings pure.*

When I went to see K towards the end, he said: *Come and visit me every day.* But I didn't, because he was so weak and I didn't want to disturb him.

Until the final moment, his mind was clear. I saw him for the last time three days before his death. He said to me: *Je suis en train de partir, vous comprenez? (I am leaving, you understand?)* These were his last words to me.

On the night of K's death, I felt an enveloping wave of peace flood gently but powerfully through the valley with the brilliant moonlight.

An extraordinary space in the mind

You see, death is destruction. It is final; you can't argue with it. You can't say, "No, wait a few days more." You can't discuss; you can't plead; it is final; it is absolute. We never face anything final, absolute. We always go around it, and that is why we dread death. We can invent ideas, hopes, fears, and have beliefs such as "we are going to be resurrected, be born again" – those are all the cunning ways of the mind, hoping for a continuity, which is of time, which is not a fact, which is merely of thought. You know, when I talk about death, I am not talking about your death or my death – I am talking about *death*, that extraordinary phenomenon.

… So when we talk about death, we are not talking about your death or my death. It does not really very much matter if you die or I die; we are going to die, happily or in misery – die happily, having lived fully, completely, with every sense, with all our being, fully alive, in full health, or die like miserable people crippled with age, frustrated, in sorrow, never knowing a day, happy, rich, never having a moment in which we have seen the sublime. So I am talking about Death, not about the death of a particular person.

… If you have cut everything around you – every psychological root, hope, despair, guilt, anxiety, success, attachment – then

Near Pepper Tree Retreat (Arya Vihara) in Ojai, California

out of this operation, this denial of this whole structure of society, not knowing what will happen to you when you are operating completely, out of this total denial there is the energy to face that which you call death.

… You see, we do not love. Love comes only when there is nothing, when you have denied the whole world – not an enormous thing called "the world" but just your world, the little world in which you live – the family, the attachment, the quarrels, the domination, your success, your hopes, your guilts, your obediences, your gods, and your myths. When you deny all that world, when there is absolutely nothing left, no gods, no hopes, no despairs, when there is no seeking, then out of that great emptiness comes love, which is an extraordinary reality, which is an extraordinary fact not conjured up by the mind, the mind which has a continuity with the family through sex, through desire.

And if you have no love – which is really the unknown – do what you will, the world will be in chaos. Only when you deny totally the known – what you know, your experiences, your knowledge, not the technological knowledge but the knowledge of your ambitions, your experiences, your family – when you deny the known completely, when you wipe it away, when you die to all that, you will see that there is an extraordinary emptiness, an extraordinary space in the mind. And it is only that space that knows what it is to love. And it is only in that space that there is creation – not the creation of children or putting a painting on canvas, but that creation that is the total energy, the unknowable. But to come to that, you must die to everything that you have known. And in that dying, there is great beauty, there is inexhaustible life energy.

On Living and Dying, pp. 100–02
6th talk, Bombay, 7 March 1962
© 1992 Krishnamurti Foundation Trust Ltd
and Krishnamurti Foundation of America

A full-grown century plant (Agave americana) in Ojai

POSTSCRIPT

Twenty-eight years have passed since Krishnamurti's death. The 100th anniversary of his birth was celebrated in 1995 by the Foundations, an opportunity to give his work more exposure.

The Dalai Lama inaugurated a gathering at Vasanta Vihar that was attended by several thousand people; speakers included Pupul Jayakar and the former President of India, R. Venkataraman. A large gathering was also held in Ojai. Universities in Mexico, the USA and France held conferences on Krishnamurti. New books were published, among them the comprehensive work by Evelyne Blau titled *Krishnamurti: 100 Years.*

During his lifetime, K frequently asked those around him: *What are you going to do when K is gone?* At times he pointed out that groups that had formed around a leader tended to break apart within forty years of the leader's death. He also often emphasized the shortcomings and even dangers of organizations that follow a particular leader and maintain a hierarchical structure.

When the trustees would answer K's question with, We will protect and disseminate the teachings, K would say: *If you live the teachings, then they will spread.* And: *The teachings have their own protection.* He also invited them to listen to the teachings, and therefore delve into the questions being explored, as they would draw water from a well: with a large bucket rather than a small cup.

There are four Krishnamurti Foundations and over forty Committees in various countries around the world, all engaged in preserving and making known the beauty and urgency of

Krishnamurti's teachings. For many years I used to liaise as closely as I could with the people involved in these groups and visited many of them, some of them often. In 1992 I began to work with former Brockwood staff members, initially so that my interactions with the School and the Foundation there might be more effective, then increasingly in order that the same might be true for my interactions with the Schools and Foundations elsewhere. There are now seven of us working in this way. We call ourselves Krishnamurti Link International (KLI), named after The Link, a publication we printed for many years. Four of us are or were trustees of one or other of the K Foundations,[54] and one of us helped to start kinfonet.org.

The Foundations continue to maintain the Schools, Study Centres and Archives; they publish books and periodicals, produce MP3 recordings and DVDs, have websites, arrange for the translation of all of this material into numerous languages, and organize various presentations and gatherings. The Committees help the Foundations with their work, assisting with translations and distribution of the many publications in various media.

A newer endeavour of the Foundations is jkrishnamurti.org, the official online archive of the teachings. At the end of 2013, this website was making freely available, in English, 1,800 text documents, 158 video files, 96 audio files and 18 full books – plus more in Spanish, Portuguese, Italian, Chinese, French, Greek, Dutch and German; Russian and Arabic will be added. All of this is now part of a larger website covering all of the Foundations, their activities and online stores, developed with help from

---

54 I am an emeritus trustee of KFT, an honorary trustee of KFA and a former trustee of KFI.

Vishwanath Alluri[55]. It will make the teachings of Krishnamurti available on tablets and smartphones while staying in tune with ever-changing technologies.

There is also the Complete Teachings Project, a long-term endeavour to collect the entire body of K's work into a coherently edited master reference.

The Schools, too, are developing strongly, with two new educational centres established in India since K's death: Sahyadri School near Pune, and Pathashaala south of Chennai. Teacher education is also progressing. One of the initial steps was taken by Ahalya Chari[56] with the *Journal of the Krishnamurti Schools*. Now Alok Mathur[57] and Gopal Krishnamurthy[58] are designing modules, conferences and seminars for teachers and others based on K's approach to education. Gopal hopes to collaborate with the University of California Santa Barbara and Winchester University in developing a college-level certification programme.

---

55 Vishwanath Alluri was a Rishi Valley student; his son and daughter were students at Brockwood. He is an industry-awarded founder of IMImobile and a trustee of both KFT and KFI. He helps the Foundations in many ways, especially with projects – like JKOnline – that need technical expertise.

56 Ahalya Chari contributed to newly independent India's education system, then joined Rajghat Besant School in 1976. In 1982 she became head of The School in Chennai. She began the *Journal of the Krishnamurti Schools* and edited each issue until her death in 2013, at the age of 92.

57 Alok Mathur has long been a teacher at Rishi Valley School. He is now Head of Rishi Valley Institute for Teacher Education, and a trustee of KFI.

58 Gopal Krishnamurthy was a student at Rishi Valley, The Valley School and Brockwood, and taught at CFL, Brockwood and Oak Grove. He is currently Director of Academics at Brockwood. He is also the director of teacher education programmes held in various parts of the world under the title 'Re-Envisioning Education' and 'The Art, Science and Craft of Teaching and Learning'.

Autumn fields near Brockwood Park

K was concerned about what would happen with the Foundations once he was gone. It was one of his deep intentions that all of the Foundations and Schools would feel as one and that they would work together in that spirit. He communicated this repeatedly to those who worked with him during his long life. The Foundations now meet every year and a half for International Trustees Meetings and they cooperate extensively. In fact, it seems to me that they, along with many others, are working together now more than ever.

It is our earth, not yours or mine

Why is there, one must ask, this division – the Russian, the American, the British, the French, the German and so on – why is there this division between man and man, between race and race, culture against culture, one series of ideologies against another? Why? Why is there this separation? Man has divided the earth as yours and mine – why? Is it that we try to find security, self-protection, in a particular group, or in a particular belief, faith? For religions also have divided man, put man against man – the Hindus, the Muslims, the Christians, the Jews and so on. Nationalism, with its unfortunate patriotism, is really a glorified form, an ennobled form, of tribalism. In a small tribe or in a very large tribe there is a sense of being together, having the same language, the same superstitions, the same kind of political, religious system. And one feels safe, protected, happy, comforted. And for that safety, comfort, we are willing to kill others who have the same kind of desire to be safe, to feel protected, to belong to something. This terrible desire to identify oneself with a group, with a flag, with a religious ritual and so on, gives us the feeling that we have roots, that we are not homeless wanderers. There is the desire, the urge, to find one's roots.

And also we have divided the world into economic spheres, with all their problems. Perhaps one of the major causes of war is heavy industry. When industry and economics go hand in hand with politics they must inevitably sustain a separative activity to maintain their economic stature. All countries are doing this, the great and the small. The small are being armed by the big nations – some quietly, surreptitiously, others openly. Is the cause of all this misery, suffering, and the enormous waste of money on armaments, the visible sustenance of pride, of wanting to be superior to others?

It is our earth, not yours or mine or his. We are meant to live on it, helping each other, not destroying each other. This is not some romantic nonsense but the actual fact. But man has divided the earth, hoping thereby that in the particular he is going to find happiness, security, a sense of abiding comfort.

Until a radical change takes place and we wipe out all nationalities, all ideologies, all religious divisions, and establish a global relationship – psychologically first, inwardly before organizing the outer – we shall go on with wars. If you harm others, if you kill others, whether in anger or by organized murder which is called war, you, who are the rest of humanity, not a separate human being fighting the rest of mankind, are destroying yourself.

Krishnamurti to Himself
entry of 31 March 1983
© 1987 Krishnamurti Foundation Trust Ltd

APPENDIX 1

The Core of Krishnamurti's Teaching

Written by Krishnamurti in 1980 at the request of his biographer Mary Lutyens

The core of Krishnamurti's teaching is contained in the statement he made in 1929 when he said "Truth is a pathless land." Man cannot come to it through any organization, through any creed, through any dogma, priest or ritual, nor through any philosophical knowledge or psychological technique. He has to find it through the mirror of relationship, through the understanding of the contents of his own mind, through observation and not through intellectual analysis or introspective dissection.

Man has built in himself images as a fence of security – religious, political, personal. These manifest as symbols, ideas, beliefs. The burden of these images dominates man's thinking, his relationships, and his daily life. These images are the causes of our problems for they divide man from man. His perception of life is shaped by the concepts already established in his mind. The content of his consciousness is his entire existence. The individuality is the name, the form and superficial culture he acquires from tradition and environment. The uniqueness of man does not lie in the superficial but in complete freedom from the content of his consciousness, which is common to all humanity. So he is not an individual.

Freedom is not a reaction; freedom is not choice. It is man's pretence that because he has choice he is free. Freedom is pure observation without direction, without fear of punishment and reward. Freedom is without motive; freedom is not at the end of the evolution of man but lies in the first step of his existence. In observation one begins to discover the lack of freedom. Freedom is found in the choiceless awareness of our daily existence and activity.

Thought is time. Thought is born of experience and knowledge, which are inseparable from time and the past. Time is the psychological enemy of man. Our action is based on knowledge and therefore time, so man is always a slave to the past. Thought is ever limited and so we live in constant conflict and struggle. There is no psychological evolution. When man becomes aware of the movement of his own thoughts, he will see the division between the thinker and thought, the observer and the observed, the experiencer and the experience. He will discover that this division is an illusion. Then only is there pure observation which is insight without any shadow of the past or of time. This timeless insight brings about a deep, radical mutation in the mind.

Total negation is the essence of the positive. When there is negation of all those things that thought has brought about psychologically, only then is there love, which is compassion and intelligence.

J. Krishnamurti
© 1980 Krishnamurti Foundation Trust Ltd

The Study Centres

Dictated by Krishnamurti to a Trustee of the Foundation at Vasanta Vihar, Chennai on 26 January 1984

It must last a thousand years, unpolluted, like a river that has the capacity to cleanse itself, which means no authority whatsoever for the inhabitants. And the teachings in themselves have the authority of the Truth.

It is a place for the flowering of goodness: a communication and cooperation not based on work, ideal or personal authority. Cooperation implies not round some object or principle, belief and so on. As one comes to the place, each one in his work – working in the garden or doing something – may discover something, a fact as he is working. And he communicates and has a dialogue with the other inhabitants – to be questioned, doubted and to see the weight of the truth of his discovery. So there is a constant communication and not a solitary achievement, a solitary enlightenment or understanding. It is the responsibility of each one to bring this about in this sense: that each one of us, if he discovers something basic, anew, it is not personal, but it is for all people who are there.

It is not a community. The very word *community* or *commune* is an aggressive or separative movement from the whole of humanity. But it does not mean that the whole humanity comes into this place. It is essentially a religious centre according to what K has said about religion. It is a place where not only is one physically active but there is a sustained and continuous inward watching.

The Krishnamurti Centre at Brockwood Park

So there is a movement of learning where each one becomes the teacher and the disciple. It is not a place for one's own illumination or one's own goal of fulfillment, artistically, religiously, or in any way, but rather sustaining each other and nourishing each other in flowering in goodness.

There must be absolute freedom from orthodox or traditional movements. But rather there must be total freedom, absolute freedom from all sense of nationalities, racial prejudices, religious beliefs and faiths. If one is not capable of doing this with honesty and integrity, he had better keep away from this place. Essentially one has the insight to see that knowledge is the enemy of man.

This is not a place for romanticists, sentimentalists or emotion. This requires a good brain, which does not mean intellectual, but rather a brain that is objective, fundamentally honest to itself, and has integrity in word and deed.

A dialogue is very important. It is a form of communication in which question and answer continues till a question is left without an answer. Thus the question is suspended between two persons involved in this answer and question. It is like a bud which untouched, blossoms. If the question is left totally untouched by thought, it then has its own answer because the questioner and answerer, as persons, have disappeared. This is a form of dialogue in which investigation reaches a certain point of intensity and depth, which then has a quality which thought can never reach. It is not a dialectical investigation of opinions, ideas, but rather exploration by two or many serious, good brains.

This place must be of great beauty, with trees, birds and quietness, for beauty is truth, and truth is goodness and love. The external beauty, external tranquility, silence, may affect the inner tranquility, but the environment must in no way influence the inner beauty. Beauty can only be when the self is not. The environment, which must have great wonder, must in no way be an absorbing factor, like a toy with a child. Here, there are no toys but inner depth, substance and integrity that are not put together by thought. Knowledge is not beauty. Beauty is love, and where there is knowledge there is no beauty.

The depth of the question brings its own right answer. All this is not an intellectual entertainment, a pursuit of theories. The word is the deed. The two must never be separate. Where the word is the deed, that is integrity.

Intelligence can only be where there is love and compassion. Compassion can never exist where the brain is conditioned or has an anchorage. A collection of mediocrities does not make a religious centre. A religious centre demands the highest quality in everything that one is doing, and the highest capacity of the brain. The full meaning of mediocrity is a dull, heavy brain, drugged by knowledge.

The flowering of goodness is not an ideal to be pursued or sought after, as a goal in the future. We are not setting up a utopia, but rather dealing with hard facts. You can make all this into something to be achieved in the future. The future is the present. The present is the past and the future, the whole structure of thought and time. But if one lives with death, not occasionally but every day, there is no change. Change is strife and the pain of anxiety. As there is no collection, accumulation of knowledge, there is no change because one is living with death continuously.

The first stone we lay should be religious.

J. Krishnamurti
© 1984 Krishnamurti Foundation Trust Ltd

About *Krishnamurti's Notebook* – A Book Review

Brockwood Park, 19 June 1976

A book review of *Krishnamurti's Notebook* was published today in the *Guardian* newspaper. It was written by Angela Neustatter and was an undistinguished one. Krishnamurti didn't read it through but gathered it was nothing and said, "I will review it". He then dictated to me a splendid review, laughing as he went along.

Two days later on 21 June he and I went to London and lunched with Mary Lutyens. She was given the review which Krishnaji had written, but not told her. While she read it he watched with a merry look. She didn't guess where it came from. At the end she asked and was told and there was much laughter.

Mary Zimbalist

Krishnamurti's Notebook – A Book Review by J. Krishnamurti himself

Brockwood Park, 20 June 1976

Aldous Huxley wrote that to listen to Krishnamurti was like listening to the Buddha, perhaps the greatest teacher in the world. When Aldous Huxley said it it was in all seriousness, for he was a very serious man. I had met him several times with

Krishnamurti in California, when his first wife was living, and often in London and Rome. He was an extraordinary man. He could talk about music, the modern and the classical, he could explain in great detail science and its effect on modern civilisation and of course he was quite familiar with the philosophies, Zen, Vedanta and naturally Buddhism. To go for a walk with him was a delight. He would discourse on the wayside flowers and, though he couldn't see properly, whenever we passed in the hills of California an animal fairly close by, he would name it and develop the destructive nature of modern civilisation and its violence. We used to go for walks with Krishnamurti, who would help him to cross a stream or a pothole. These two had a strange relationship with each other, affectionate, considerate and it seemed a non-verbal communication. They would often be sitting together without saying a word. And so when I was asked to write something about Krishnamurti and to review *Krishnamurti's Notebook* I was more than glad to do this for I respected them both enormously.

Anyone who wishes to write a review of a book of this kind must have considerable knowledge of Hindu expression of the realization of truth and have explored deeply into Buddhism. Onc of thc great teachers of Buddhism was Nagarjuna who taught total negation. Buddhism has been broken up into two separate schools, the North and the South—Mahayana and Hinayana which is Theravada. It seems to me that Krishnamurti is much closer to the Buddha and beyond Nagarjuna than perhaps to the Hindu expression of truth. *Krishnamurti's Notebook* appears to me to go beyond the Upanishads and Vedanta. When he talks about knowledge and the ending of it, it is in essence Vedanta, which literally means the ending of knowledge. But the Vedantists and their followers in different parts of the world are really maintaining the structure of knowledge, perhaps thinking knowledge is salvation, as most scientists do.

Tradition has such a strong grip on the mind that few seem to escape its tentacles and I think this is where Krishnamurti begins. He constantly asserts that freedom is the first and last step. The traditionalists maintain that a highly disciplined mind is necessary for freedom: be a slave first and afterwards you will be free. To Krishnamurti what seems the most important thing, and he had repeated this in all his talks and dialogues, is that there must be freedom to observe, not some ideological freedom but freedom from the very knowledge and experience which has been acquired yesterday. This brings about a tremendous problem. If there is no knowledge of many yesterdays, then what is it that is capable of observing? If knowledge is not the root of observation, what have you with which to observe? Can the many yesterdays be totally forgotten, which is the essence of freedom? He maintains that it can. This is possible only when the past ends in the present, meeting it fully, head-on. The past, as he asserts, is the ego, the structure of the 'me' which prevents total observation.

An ordinary person reading this book – if he will ever read it – will inevitably cry out, saying, What are you talking about? To him Krishnamurti explains very carefully in manifold ways the necessary memory and the psychological memory. Knowledge is necessary to function in any field of our daily life but psychological memory of our hurts, anxiety, pain and sorrow is the factor of division and hence there is a conflict between the essential knowledge which is required to drive a car and the experience as knowledge which is the whole movement of the psyche. He points out this fact in relationship, in our fragmented ways of life, the ideal and the actual. I have read this book very carefully. I am familiar with the Upanishads and have delved deeply into the teachings of the Buddha. I am fairly familiar with the psychological studies of modern times. As far as I have come in my studies I have not found the phrase 'the observer is the observed', with

Adyar Beach, where K was 'discovered', in Madras (Chennai)

its full meaning. Perhaps some ancient thinker may have said it, but one of the most important things that Krishnamurti has found is this great truth which, when it actually takes place, as it has occasionally happened to me personally, literally banishes the movement of time. Let me add here that I am not a follower nor do I accept Krishnamurti as my guru. To him the idea of becoming a guru is an abomination. With critical examination I find this book totally absorbing because he annihilates everything that thought has put together. It is a shocking thing when one realises this. It is a real physical shock.

Can a human being live in this state of absolute nothingness except for his daily bread and work – in the total emptiness of consciousness as we know it? As Krishnamurti points out over and over again, consciousness is the movement of all thought. Thought is matter, measurable, and thought is time, which implies that psychologically there is no tomorrow. That means no hope. This is a devastating psychological fact and our everyday mind is not only shocked by this statement but probably will refuse to examine it closely. It is death now. From this death arises a totally different quality of energy, of a different dimension, inexhaustible and without an end. He says this is the ultimate benediction.

I can feel through all the pages of this book a sense of extraordinary love which the Tibetans might call the love or the compassion of the Bodhisattva, but when you give it a name and an ideological symbol you will lose the perfume. It has strangely affected my life. I am not a Christian or a Buddhist, I don't belong to any of these categories. In my youth I was a Communist – not a card-carrying one – but I was enamoured of no class, government withering away and so on. It enticed me for a couple of years but I saw what was actually happening and was utterly disillusioned with it all. So I turned to the investigation of my own misery and that of another. Christianity had little to offer in this direction and so I moved to the Orient. You may remember the story when someone came to the Buddha in tears on account of a death. He told her to find a single house where death had not been. It was not because there was a death close to me but death meant sorrow. The ancient Egyptians sought immortality in perpetuating matter. This may be a superficial conclusion but they sought a continuity of life as they knew it. This question of immortality comes to an end when, as Krishnamurti points out, time stops. When that actually takes place there is a state, according to him, in which there is no beginning and no ending. And that perhaps is the immortal.

It is curious also how he deals with meditation. Meditation, according to him, can never be a conscious thing, and one can see the reason for this. If one meditates purposefully with a deliberate intention, consciousness then continues with all its content. All this does sound rather exalted and unrealistic but it is not.

Krishnamurti and I have met very often recently and in the past when Aldous Huxley was with him. He puts it all in very clear words, logically, and he suddenly jumps forward and you have to race after him, but what he is saying is so accurate and clear. And if you, the reader, are really concerned with the whole problem of existence I would highly recommend that you get hold of this book and others by him and spend some time with them. I have found in these books not only a sense of love and great beauty, but something far beyond all this. It is like spending some time with yourself, watching our idiocies, our aspirations and failures and if you pursue them factually, that is totally real and all-consuming.

J. Krishnamurti
© Krishnamurti Foundation Trust Ltd

INDEX OF NAMES

Some other 'memories of Krishnamurti'

Blau, Evelyne
Krishnamurti: 100 Years
Stewart, Tabori & Chang, New York, 1995

Field, Sidney
Krishnamurti: The Reluctant Messiah
Paragon House, New York, 1989

Holroyd, Stuart
Quest of the Quiet Mind
Aquarian Press, Wellingborough, 1980

Holroyd, Stuart
Krishnamurti: The Man, The Mystery & The Message
Element, Shaftesbury & Rockport, 1991

Jayakar, Pupul
Krishnamurti: A Biography
Harper & Row, New York, 1986

Krishna, Padmanabhan
A Jewel on a Silver Platter
Peepal Leaves, 2015

Krohnen, Michael
The Kitchen Chronicles: 1001 Lunches with J. Krishnamurti
Edwin House, Ojai, 1997

Lee, R. E. Mark
Knocking at the Open Door: My Years with J. Krishnamurti
Hay House, New Delhi, 2014

Lutyens, Mary
Krishnamurti: The Years of Awakening
John Murray, London, 1975

Lutyens, Mary
Krishnamurti: The Years of Fulfilment
John Murray, London, 1983

Lutyens, Mary
Krishnamurti: The Open Door
John Murray, London, 1988

Lutyens, Mary
   The Life and Death of Krishnamurti
   John Murray, London, 1990

Moody, David Edmund
   The Unconditioned Mind – J. Krishnamurti and the Oak Grove School
   Quest Books, Wheaton, Illinois, 2011

Narayan, G.
   As the River Joins the Ocean – Reflections about J. Krishnamurti
   Edwin House, Ojai, 1998

Patwardhan, Sunanda
   A Vision of the Sacred – My Personal Journey with Krishnamurti
   Edwin House, Ojai, 1999

Smith, Ingram
   The Transparent Mind – A Journey with Krishnamurti
   Edwin House, Ojai, 1999

Vernon, Roland
   Star in the East – Krishnamurti: The Invention of a Messiah
   Constable, London, 2000

Zimbalist, Mary
   Online at inthepresenceofk.org